Misty Mountain Musings

Misty Mountain Musings

NICHOLAS MICHAEL MORROW
Drawings by Sally Rutledge
and Ami Spangler

MISTY MOUNTAIN
PUBLISHING
2022

Copyright © 2022 by Nicholas Michael Morrow

All rights reserved. Printed in the United States of America. No part of this book may be used or reproduced in any manner whatsoever without written permission except in the case of brief quotations embodied in critical articles or reviews.
For permissions contact: Nicholas Morrow at
mistymountainarts@nym.hush.com

Published by:
Misty Mountain Publishing
Yelm, Washington, USA
mistymountainarts.com

Misty Mountain Publishing is dedicated to the publication, promotion, and performance of inspirational poetry and art.

Cover images by Nicholas Morrow
Interior images by Sally Rutledge and Ami Spangler

Print ISBN: 978-0-9787977-1-3

Musing: reflection or thought in the gesture of poetry and prose entangled with a playful imagination.

1. Poetry. 2. Inspirational Poetry. 3. Imagination. 4. Mysticism. 5. Musings. 6. Initiation. I. Title

First Edition: September 2022

Dear Readers

Imagine these musings as observations
from the bank of a river
that flows to the sea.

The lifetimes we live have continuity
and the human beings we meet have been with us before
incarnating with purpose to experience along the way.

We are poet and muse,
inspiring word, verse, and rhyme.
May these musings do us justice
knowing we are honored
each to each Beloved.

To
Marianna Lands

Welcome

I have prepared a feast for this occasion. This is no ordinary cuisine, touting many courses, tastes, and pleasures. The consciousness that weaves the pristine web scribed with a poet's heart is drawn from a multiplicity of beings evolving in the moment that is always on the move.

Contemplate the drawings as you do a sunrise or birdsong with fragrance wafting on the breeze, or when confronted by a metaphor playing in musical space.

We are poets and the muse is life on both sides of the river with poetry the bridge linking our destinies. Join me on this adventure with light heart, lucid mind, and good will.

Contents

WELCOME i

SECTION 1: PLACE 1

SECTION 2: ART 25

SECTION 3: HUMAN 49

SECTION 4: ANTIDOTE 73

SECTION 5: HOVERING 99

SECTION 6: AGE 123

SECTION 7: HOME 147

INDEX OF TITLES 169

A CONVERSATION AT THE
SOUTHSIDE COFFEE CAFÉ 175

ACKNOWLEDGEMENTS 181

SHORT BIOGRAPHIES 182

SECTIONS

Seven Spheres
The Quest and Grail
Illuminating The Darkness
And The Human Being
Creator and Creation

1

Place

Earth, Air, Fire, Water
And A Finer Substance
Begetting Form
The Earth Where We Dwell
Beneath The Sun

The Pacific Northwest

On the vast Texas plain where the sky is big
revealing the Earth's gentle undulations
and on the desert plateau of New Mexico
where the stars are so bright
that it seems you could touch them,
are the places where I have lived
most of my long, delicious life.

Now I live in the Pacific Northwest
between the ocean and Mount Rainier,
often boasting a crown of whimsical clouds
or hidden in mist and pearlescence
as if engaged in Delphian mystery.

The sun rarely shines here in winter
and the stars make their merry round
almost forgotten, save in memories
when I gazed into their world,
sharing the dance.

Life here is rich and pervasive
and it will mesmerize or devour you
unless you meet it with the clarity
of inspired thought and deed
that behind the hovering mantle of gray
is more vibrant than on desert plateaus.

Between the mountain and the sea
a gentle wind, mist and rain come and go,
like a pendulum in perpetual motion
blending dawn and dusk into a singularity
without beginning or end.

The muse however is undaunted,
celebrating winter and casting her spell
with imagination, hope, or omen,
whispering in the poet's ear
incantations dressed for the occasion
entertaining us on long winter nights.

THE BEACH HOUSE

In my dream I walk upon a deserted beach
warm from the sun suspended in a blue sky
and comb through countless treasures from the sea.
I watch the gulls as they sweep the waves
diving from time to time, screeching
as they compete for the prize.

The waves swell, curl, and tumble,
wash onto the shore and return,
the wind joining in fastidious harmony,
bending the grass and sculpting the trees
that appear as chimeras between worlds
reflecting the manifold moods in me.

On a rise protected from the shifting sands
is a grey weathered house overlooking the sea.
It must have grown from the same dream
that since my youth has called me here
to witness the majesty and play of light
that dances like diamonds on the waves
and breathe the salty air.

In the night a foghorn sounds, deep and slow,
with primal groan and warning –

*"Beware of the unseen dangers veiled in darkness
lest you be cast ashore as food or treasure!"*

The voices of wind and wave rise and fall,
several octaves running along the shore,
while a panorama of myth and legend spreads
from horizon to horizon in a stary sky
proclaiming with hope and intimations
what has been and will be.

If you can hear me, join me for a season
at my beach house overlooking the sea
to partake of the beauty and delight it offers,
walking on warm sand and riding the waves,
young, innocent, and free,
dreaming no more.

LOVE IS ALWAYS THE PRIZE

These musings came to or through me
with inspirations that I cannot claim
and their source only sometimes identify.
I do not sit and write with an idea
but a feeling maybe or mood,
followed by words that move me
to pick up my journal and begin,
laid upon the page without effort.

Poetry flows like a river through the soul
that abides in the poet's breast
with a voice that is unique for every poet.
It could be that a poet speaks the same poem
with different words, message, and design,
many poems in one and never done,
like life with its seasons
has beginning, duration, and end,
returning with a similar presence,
hopefully more evolved and refined.

May these musings be companion and confidant
through the mist to the summit for a majestic view,
revealing the mysteries that are yours to behold
without indigestion from the spicy ingredients
or truths you would rather not know.

Beauty comes in myriad forms
goodness sometimes in disguise,
prayer, subtle or explicit is a quest,
and love is free my friend, for love is always the prize,
with hope, joy, and delight as a blessing.

Dawn and Dusk

Dawn and dusk
with sunlit days and star studded nights
exchanging places in a sumptuous dance
keeping time with love to open the door
and courage to dream different than before.

You and I surrender to the moment,
synchronized with the pulse of earthly rhythms,
hand in hand on a mountain path in summer,
in each other's arms by a fire in winter,
the outer world clothed in crystal essence.

Love lifts us beyond everyday mortality
stilling our longing for what could have been,
while sun, moon, and stars orchestrate
another chapter in the saga of evolution.

When we wake we find the scene set,
scripts assigned to each in their turn,
taking our places upon the stage
with a cosmos gathered round.

The curtains rise and our eyes meet
with recognition of who we are,
welcoming the synchronicity.

Newborn Sun

The grip of night holds sway,
yet, a difference, faint, almost imperceptible,
maybe imagined or hoped for is in the air,
darkness surrendering to the inevitable,
resentment realizing its task is fruitless.
Light but a glimmer stirs in the depths
loosening the veil and illusion of separateness
that the eye creates to apprehend her lover,
a reflection in destiny's magic mirror.

No matter how great the pain or resistance
desire for love is greater, dissolving hesitation,
healing the past and opening.
In the valley and cave of our heart we reside,
held by mountains that pierce the sky,
rooted in the Earth as an anchor
for being and expression.

We are blessed with the task
to build community where everyone is welcome
confronting the demons that bar the way,
as human beings become warriors
with the sting of karma set aside.

We prepare for a golden dawn,
the light within a glow and anticipation,
thirteen holy nights, cycles repeating, turning,
a cosmic ritual with candles upon the alter lit,
gifts given and received, realized and set free.

Although the dark night is still upon us,
the light grows strong, the seasons rich,
the fruit beautiful, the love pure
as a Newborn Sun.

The Temple

The temple is here and there.
We pursue the truth wherever we go.
Someday everyone will know the difference
experiencing the infinite in everything.

What are we attached to but identity
with purpose for being and becoming?
The temple appears and we appreciate her beauty,
care for her gardens and celebrate the word.
Mansions rise and fall, each built brick by brick,
and we participate until we understand.

Aroused by desire, accepting the call, we return
to nurture love in the world and in our innocence
build the temple one more time knowing it will fall.
We stand at the threshold of destruction
with hope and labor as our offering,
the last brick in hand paying for grace.

Will the temple be hidden midst the chaos?
Will old, lifeless forms fall away
with new ones to express our love?

Cycles draw to a close without a conclusion
and are born anew to receive our contribution.

The Pinnacle

From a pinnacle of ancient moss covered stone
the valley spreads before you with towering
snow-capped mountains beyond.

Surrendering to the enchantment, you are swept away,
far, far away from the concerns of life,
expanding to merge with ethereal beings
inspired with hope for the future
and a subtle urgency that cannot be denied,
seeming but a dream from the pinnacle
where you pray.

It is winter and a cold wind haunts the cliffs.
The sun, suspended in a blue sky,
warms you and holds you in her embrace.
There is balance in this world
and you will bring balance to the dream.
The heart and soul of humanity
engaged with the adversaries of awakening
will find balance and direction as well
and you will never be alone.

The brown Earth that lies below
will be green, teeming with life in spring,
and her creatures will reappear, celebrating return,
while the mountains covered in snow
promise abundance for the seasons to follow,
and you will be given guidance
with courage for the journey.

Night In Winter

The night is grey and moist
beckoning the dawn that is grey as well,
the air teeming with fragrance from the sea.
The birds do not sing much in winter
yet frolic at the feeder outside my window,
somehow aware that I am watching
and this is their way of giving thanks
before they disappear into the grey
that hides their wintery abode.

Few sounds emanate from the elemental world
save the wind that blows from the sea
to the mountain or from mountain to sea,
like a bard whispering vague incantations
of the affairs in nature's kingdoms and beyond.
When it snows the hush is deeper than death,
a great white silence, beautiful and pervasive.

The road however wakes before dawn
as cars beat the wet pavement
carrying their occupants to perform their duty
honoring necessity with purpose and sacrifice.

I am awed at the courage and will it takes
to wake in darkness and travel somewhere,
returning in darkness when done,
hopefully greeted as heroes to a warm fire
appreciated and dearly loved.

For me long winter nights inspire the muse
fostering a mood for creativity and communion,
imagination giving its essence to the word,
while cosmic beings celebrate the season
and cloak the day with grey luminescence
cold to the bone.

A Midwinter's Tale

It is a cold moonlit night in midwinter.
You come in silence and secrecy,
spruce, cedar, and pine silhouetted in a grey sky,
frozen, still, like hair on a beggar's back
caught in supplication and prayer
with its host in another world
beyond dream or death or identity.

It is the beggar who tells this story,
so I entreat You, dear friend,

"What do You hear?"

Not words, I know, for in this world
there are no words or images to share,
or others who know corporality like You and I,
or longing to break the silence,
or warmth to melt the ice and stir the air.

In this emptiness there is nothing,
no one save I who knows not that I am,
without substance, time, or space for company,
and if You can hear me, be my witness.

I have loved, touched, and betrayed,
seeing all in bitter truth and clarity –
the selfish, lustful need for artistic deeds,
beauty and fame with my name written there,
the lips of a lover whispering sweet intimacy
giving their heart for one more night in paradise,
while I take it all, leaving tokens for remembrance
devastating innocence and never looking back.

Maybe You should not come, not yet,
because I am not ready and everything would be the same –
You and I tasting the sweetness and fearing it will end,
creating boundaries and chains to hold it fast,
securing it with a lock without a key.

We know how that will turn out,
this tale told in every epoch, cycle, and season,
for nothing is ever still, save this grey place
where neither dark nor light can enter
or time move or space create.

Memory both sweet and bitter lingers
recreating the tale again and again,
and if there is such a thing as evolution
it will reveal itself with subtle nuance,
shifting each time the tale is told.

Who this storyteller is I do not know
because there is no one here but me.

What Do We See

What do we see when the sun rises in early spring?
What lives and weaves in fields of green?
Who are the playful entities that dance and sing
amongst the grasses as they sway with the breeze,
or in the cat upon my lap purring as I stroke her soft fur,
or in the voice of barking dogs or mournful moos of Daisy
calling to let me know she is ready for her special treat,
knowing that more than what appears is happening –
a symphony of life animated by soul and spirit
with elemental beings behind the scenes.

Human beings with a more complex presence confront us
with attitude and belief that at first seem benign,
yet, with time exerts itself with blatant or subtle control
accompanied by patterns of behavior
with a story woven into every aspect of life,
in daily rhythms, stormy days or restless nights,
saying, yes or no, this way or that, refusing to surrender
to the joy of being without agenda.

Where does the focus lie –
in the world as it appears
or in feeling that emanates from the soul
or in the I that chooses and directs?
No matter how much we contemplate the mystery
it remains aloof, coy and irresistible.

However, You and I in cherished moments of grace
can simply be without questioning,
sharing nights of splendor
and the beauty this world brings.

TOUCHING THE UNTOUCHABLE

Our journey is like a spiral in time,
center untouched, sacred and free,
strands of light forming an intricate web
where we meet and live the story
flowing like a river to our destiny.

The unknown looms before us,
feeding our fear as we enter the fray,
victory and defeat sharing the glory,
form begetting form and dissipating,
living between the lines without restraint
knowing this soon will be memory.

None the less we embrace the opportunity
and it gives us hope and courage to act
with the possibility of error along the way.
None the less we weave the web one more time
with an inclination for romance,
picking up the pieces and loving more,
a never ending story with precious moments.

Upon sacred ground we tread
walking the labyrinth from periphery to center,
placing our gifts upon the alter
in gratitude for what is and will always be,
acknowledging our relations here and there
building a bridge between worlds,
touching the untouchable.

The Quest And Grail

We know the quest and grail.
We know them well, for they are in us,
in our blood, breath, and bone,
in every thought, feeling, and deed,
spanning the realms with consequence.

How is it with You and I,
this pretentious quest leading us into the future
without prophet, hierophant, or priest to guide us,
with distractions and doubt along the way
disguised as savior and confidant to the end,
promising to join us when we come again?

Are we seekers on a quest for identity
using each other as mirrors for confirmation,
relationship with antipathy and sympathy
to keep us separate or consume?

Are we the grail for a greater quest
that seeks its destiny and liberation
beyond healing, answer, or question,
or are we the soul survivors of our race
requesting an intermission and reprieve?

Shall we choose to be a chalice
and invite the elixir to work its magic,
to look into each other's eyes with recognition
and walk hand in hand with our hearts singing
on a warm sandy beach in spring,
the sun's light on every swale and ripple,
waves washing our feet and laughing,
wave upon wave reminding us what love is –
the quest renewed when we return,
the grail a delicious memory?

We Are Free

Let us stroll, You and I,
along the shore of an inland sea on a cloudy day,
or down a shady lane with poplars piercing a blue sky,
or upon a deserted city street in the intimacy of night.

Have we met before, so familiar you seem to me?
Your eager smile and bright eyes infuse me with glee,
fresh, like dew sparkling in the morning light,
with birds singing, letting us know they agree,
a gentle breeze joining in and leaves rustling in delight,
a symphony beguiled in the spirit of serendipity.

What shall we be today –
a potter drawing a pot from native clay,
or a baker baking buns, enchanting the noses of passersby,
accompanied by fresh brewed coffee at a curb side café,
or simply ourselves in conversation sharing our dreams,
far into the future gazing, the world changing
for the better as the clock begins to toll –
"all is not as it seems!"

Now we must act or we must wait, attending to our duty
honoring commitments in the bustling life of the city,
everyone keeping time, passing us by as if we are not there.
We remember that once we were the same
living the day according to plan with endless days to follow,
and when no one seemed to care, we left.

Necessity is different for every human soul
and ours is to live each day anew
teeming with awe and wonder.

"Good morning. Have we met before?"
"The day is grey and the waves are singing a grey day song."
"Shall we stroll along the beach and join in?"
"How bright your eyes are today. Did you dream?"
"Yes. I have no plans. We are free."

THE DARK NIGHT

The night grows dark with the season,
with silence that suffers peace
more poignant than peace that follows a storm,
tempering the terror that haunts sleeping souls,
confirming that the tide has turned, receding,
leaving the beech fragrant with a feast for early risers,
returning from their dreams to devour the day.

For us there is no feast, sunrise, or golden dawn,
for the long night is still upon us,
beckoning us to follow and lending us courage
with hope for our exhausted minds and hearts,
hope without reasons why, what, or when,
or who it is that calls from the darkness
with a gentle, reassuring voice,
telling us that we will be redeemed
when the dawn finally comes.

We know they will be with us always
to guide us thorough the dark night,
for this is their task and occupation –
to accompany courageous pilgrims
who choose freedom over security,
the heart and soul of evolution.

And us, You and I, must learn to love
before the golden dawn will come,
before we can see each other in our true beauty,
and Who it is that carries us through
the dark night to greet the day.

2

ART

Alchemy Is Our Nature
And Our Gift
On One Hand
The Artist
On The Other
A Butterfly

ART AND ARTIST

What is Art –
Something crafted with the human hand,
imagination given image, shape, or form,
resonance creating music, movement in time,
a gourmet meal to be savored and consumed,
or words that tell a story, truth or fantasy,
the alchemy of spirit appearing as substance
that can be seen, touched, tasted, or heard?

Who is the Artist –
the one who creates with will and imagination,
each the other inspiring,
or the observer who experiences and beholds
the play of Gods and Humanity,
consciousness and energy from which art springs?

We gather the spoils of life both sweet and bitter
to inspire our thoughts and forge our actions
for growth midst contentment and revolution,
with the inalienable right to follow our heart,
allowing others to do the same
without fear that it agrees or disagrees.

Who do we serve? Is She human and free?
Is art a duality, a battleground for good and evil
where truth and beauty find expression,
the prodigal human returning home
alchemized, enlightened?

Are we the artist and the art?

IMAGINE

Upon the Earth we stand, feet planted on solid ground,
reaching into the star studded night, our cup held high
beckoning to beings beyond the veil,
inspiration from the lords of light,
foreboding from the angels of darkness,
imagination and intuition filling our cup
enabling voices beyond the veil to be heard,
activating the jewel in the human soul.

Whether in suffering or pleasure,
we long for what is beyond
or inside us abides and can be known,
touched and expressed with words or song.
We bow before the alter and rising,
blessed with grace and compassion,
administer the grail to hungry souls
bringing life to thought and feeling,
inspiring hands to sculpt the future,
human and divine, Earth and Heaven,
with the realms between fructified.

We are artists transmuting lead to gold,
pilgrims exploring land, sea, and inner space,
imbruing substance with warmth and reflection,
that in a distant future the Earth will be born anew,
without coming and going or duality,
beyond healing, enlightenment, and ascension,
from seed to seed.

Imagine how the Earth and we will be.

Color

Know that we know that you are a part of us,
in some ways creator, in others, our creation,
or friend, lover, and companion.
Even in the night we behold your beauty.

The mystery plays like a child in us,
enchanted by your presence, reaching with wonder
to touch your face and cannot quite,
yet we breathe and sing your many moods,
for your moods are our soul's expression.

You bless flowers with your essence,
shining midst the green with yellow, red, and violet hue,
ethereal, fleeting as in a sunset, crimson, aquamarine,
fading into cobalt and night with stars for companions
and what do I care if you are real or perception
because I could say the same for myself.

Mysteries are not to be analyzed but embraced,
as a scientist, philosopher, or artist gives you a voice
with the will to touch, heal, speak, and express.

Your gift from light comes and to light returns
through thought, feeling, and deed,
with trials and exaltation for being part of us,
as we alchemize your nature
speaking your name in our native tongue –
color, kleur, couleur, farbe, dath, colore, farge.

Color, color burning bright in our soul day and night,
in our heart, blood red like wine,
peach blossom, vermilion, and green,
shimmering in the air with translucent sheen,
gritty in earth, chestnut, ochre, and brown,
pearlescent in morning mist and rain
with pure white light for a mother.

Story

What is this story that I spin –
glory wrought from revolution, insurrection, and war,
a future where good prevails and evil meets its fate,
not destroyed but incarcerated, clasped in chains
and into a deep dark dungeon cast,
lamenting, brooding, planning a swift return,
the world organized with safeguards and restrictions
making sure that the past will not be repeated,
the dungeons with the festering, forgotten
becoming myth and legend.

You and I witness these happenings,
lives interrupted, dreams and goals cast aside
to meet the challenge that looms before us,
demanding consciousness to expose the truth,
unseen players and realms where they abide,
knowing that life and love in all things exist.

I take up sword, staff, and royal robe
according to my skills and inclination,
arm in arm with my kin, courageous, undaunted,
creating with breath, thought, and deed,
confronting evil to expose it's pernicious intent,
freed from the deep, dark dungeon
and purified in metaphoric light,
as the story unfolds with gusto and wit,
players, script, stage, and audience ready
as another chapter begins.

It is your turn to tell the story,
line by line with truth wrought words
that every being can understand.

Spin. Spin. Spin.

Intellectual Beauty and the Alchemist

Follow the recipe for making wine
and usually you will get wine,
yet, it may not always be the same
or have the same effect for every season.

Create formulas from wisdom or spirit sight
and they will hold true for most situations,
yet, we know how it is with human nature,
expecting an outcome and getting what we expect
from a formula that we meticulously follow
using pure ingredient, authenticity, and rigor.

The alchemist stirs the cauldron
with cosmic law and reason to oversee the process
towards a righteous resolution.
Yet, form and substance are not always how they appear
with name and personality sometimes a distraction,
predicting every situation before the journey begins,
and spirit with its far sighted wisdom cooperates,
the feast placed upon the table,
guests in their turn partaking.

What happens when Venus, Mercury, and Pluto appear
in the evening sky during the thirteen holy nights
and days of twenty-twenty-one and two,
with anomaly on the prowl and candles on the alter,
invocation and prayer resounding in human hearts,
casting their spell and blessing souls with levity?

Intellectual beauty and the alchemist sit at our table
with love, clarity, and truth to quench our thirst,
sharing the feast and imagining the story
without prophecy or guarantee,
presenting us with staff, star, and winged sandals
for a future we cannot see.

THE DROP

When does a drop become a pool or puddle,
and when it does, does it still feel itself a drop,
a sphere among spheres, round and full,
remembering the journey through earth, air and fire,
or raging river, catapulting, tumbling
upon and around ancient moss covered stones,
singing in a chorus from source to sea,
or in eddies as interludes observing the flow,
or still and silent upon a windless lake
mirroring mountains and trees that pierce the sky
and starry nights of sweet surrender as one escapes
leaving a fiery wake and disappearing with reverie?

The drop surrenders to experience the journey,
dispersing, becoming vapor, mist, and morning dew,
a luminous sphere on a green leaf in spring,
absorbed, consumed into chlorophyll and blood,
pulsing, keeping time with purpose and intention,
sensing life's ecstatic moments, contemplating itself,
lit up with inspiration and poetry,
romance with destiny's many moods.

Alone, upon the scorching desert sand in the final trial
annihilation transports it to the void and midnight hour,
separated from substance and form in timeless space,
until the word resounds calling her home.

Angelic beings gather to summon her essence
with divine alchemy crafting life anew,
condensed into a sphere of liquid light,
a child drop adorned with awe and wonder,
sun, wind, warmth and a human voice calling –
the etheric Christ and Sophia heart
becoming conscious of its sacred self.

Sometimes When I Pray

Sometimes when I pray there is no one to answer,
or when I listen there is only silence,
or when I seek comfort the moon grows pale
and the mind with its ongoing conversation sleeps.

I wonder why I am here
with no one to keep me company
or complain, demand, and ask questions.
With my wondering, alone in this miserable state,
I am empty of desire and identity.

When the mirror is dark I remember the beginning
when I met the muse and purpose teemed
with romance, imagination, and the word,
healing my afflictions, activating my gifts.

I cannot remember why I deserved such grace
when I was lost in the wilderness
that remained when the garden was torn asunder,
devastated with petulance, doubt, and neglect.

I could not die, unless the I that I am not died
and I remained to pick up the pieces and break the silence
with the moon at my feet and stars gathered round.

The stampede of night is given a voice
with musicians assembled and ready,
focusing on the baton held in my hand, poised,
as a single ray of light shatters the silence,
darkness surrendering to dawn and destiny,
answering my prayer.

Who Are You Beloved

Who are you Beloved,
with your many faces, attitudes, and agendas,
when mind and heart beguile us?

You are the focus of our attention
and it is you that makes us human,
yet some are unaware of your presence.
Many of your admirers sleep and dream
not knowing they dream, while others are numb.
You hold a prominent place in every heart
that perceives through the eyes of beauty.
You play your part and direct the scene,
with imagination and majesty,
in the spotlight or in the shadows,
fool, priestess, or star, hero or heroine,
an archetype for every season.

Is it love or longing that binds us
or are you so inherently a part of us
that relationship is neither truth nor fiction
with the clue a reflection in each other,
without distinction of who is who?

What a blessing the intermissions
when exhausted after a gala performance
we take time to relax and just be –
a single breathing and seeing,
a poem softly spoken.

BOUQUETS AND DIGITS

Gifts? *"Yes! I like gifts."*
A bouquet of roses? *"I accept."*
Place them in a vase arranged just so and smell them –

"Oh, how divine! Thank you. Thank you for loving me."
"What a blessing to be loved."
"What a blessing this bouquet."

Then there are gifts that in time become burdens,
crutches, distractions, not blindly to be accepted,
yet, when tossed aside they do not go away.
Even when they are buried, they putrefy.
Then, oh my, they overpower life and liberty!

Gifts, however, with gratitude must be embraced
and humanized, elevating life and all our relations,
the nature of evolution, just, wise, and amalgamated.

With age, modernity comes -

"What a pain, what a burden!"
"I just want roses and predictability"!

These strange new tools have no rhyme or reason,
or directions for use, consequence or warning.

"What do they have to do with being human?"

Still, you say, it must be so, they are here for a reason,
challenging, nay, demanding that we grow
and master their power unless it masters us.

"For what?"
"For Love of course!"

What other mystery could separate and unite us?

When digits show up on the scene
with intelligence and perfection defined
claiming power and threatening to rule,
we must take a stand, proclaiming –

"You may not enter here with your promises,
offering pleasure, peace, and leisure."
"We will not be seduced or deceived
for you are in our service,
assisting humanity to thrive and grow."

The gift accepted. *"Thank you"*

ACROSS THE THRESHOLD AND BACK AGAIN
THE THREE-FOLD STORY OF
LOVE, LIFE, AND LIGHT

Here we go, You and I, like stars in a blue-black sky,
like sunbeams on new fallen snow,
with Love that inspires human hearts to sing,
and Light that turns the good Earth green.

Glass Beads strung on a golden thread
adorn the Beloved's gown of glory,
as She dances betwixt Earth and Heaven,
You and I watching and living the story.

Whence goest thou in the star-studded night,
and where do you tarry in the brilliance of day,
and who are your devoted companions
that upon the lyre compose and play?

What constellations keep you good company?
What wave do you ride to the terrestrial shore
as you feed and nourish the one that follows
with the Ocean's heartbeat and so much more?

Three by three by three we go,
all that can be known we can know,
yet knowing is neither task nor goal,
but the pattern we make and the seeds we sow.

Some of us come from distant lands,
bringing songs and stories for bards to sing,
and some of us sustain a house and shrine
to welcome the Friend with bread and wine.

Long hours into the night we converse,
weaving tapestries of threads from our adventures,
and give our guests food for their journey,
and bid farewell with tears and laughter.

The Master opens the door when we are ready
and bids us enter without burden or mask,
to drink and assimilate the elixir of wisdom,
triumph in trials and accomplish their tasks.

Inspired, awake, over the threshold we return
with will and desire to share our wisdom
and engage in selfless acts of compassion,
speaking to the stars with heart felt words.

We live in the garden, humble, revitalized,
beauty and sentient creatures at our side,
friends and relations to share life with,
our quest complete and longing satisfied.

The Grail alone does not heal us.
Enlightenment alone does not wake us.
Adoration alone does not serve us.
Love and Friendship are gift and reward.

Three by three, Love, Life, and Light,
as it is on Earth so it is in Heaven.
Three by three, Body, Soul, and Spirit,
You and I and the World, a conversation.

Beads of Glass, like grains of sand,
possibilities held in their crystal shells,
like a seed has a cosmos within,
we are bards with stories to tell.

No Need To Dream

Deep in the world of sleep we meet
without image, voice, or face,
yet speak we do and place there is
with mood and gesture remaining
when we wake.

Clearly that world is more alive than this
where physicality is heavy, sluggish, and slow
yielding placeless, faceless phantoms
with tokens to open doors for the soul,
doors that hands cannot open or eyes enter,
bestowing riddles for heart and mind
to ponder and forget as waking returns.

Poetry is more subtle than dreaming or waking.
Read once or twice it touches the soul
with authenticity more direct and poignant
than the intellect alone can touch.

I will join You there without the necessity
for place or identity to hinder our intimacy,
bypassing law to access longing and desire,
remembering past lives and adventures
that set the stage with the script we live now,
love healing our wounds and clearing the field,
others remaining for lifetimes to come.

Joy and sorrow are tools for waking
and life is sometimes a trial we must endure
to find the jewel we are seeking,
giving it back a hundred-fold for those who follow
while You and I begin again
the blissful, tragic, and often comic journey home,
the poem present in gaze and embrace
without need for dreaming to share our intimacy,
without thought, name, or definition in the way
of this precious, sumptuous love we share.

Ultimate Surender

And so it is that global unity is upon us,
that the dissonance without disturbs the peace within
interrupting our sleep and prophesying the future.

Hearts must know, choose, and act
to survive, live and love a true love,
to confront the angels of darkness on hallowed ground
and foster an awakening for eons to come,
mastering freedom and joining forces with beauty,
confronting evil to open the darkness
so the planets and stars can shine,
speaking to each other and dancing
to music that long ago became silent,
cultivating new harmonies, celestial harmonies
within the heart of humanity –
even unto Earth where awakening takes its stand
and the ultimate surrender becomes freedom
with truth, beauty, and goodness as our guide.

Wrapped in Wit

The poet's voice, wrapped in wit,
sometimes a roar and sometimes a whisper,
more real than a grandiose landscape,
more substantial than words can tell,
for words speak both truth and fiction
and in themselves are simply light and air
caressing form with pristine vision,
sublime, sensitive, and fair,
creating worlds with the imagination
to tell of truth and beauty living there,
revealing a delicate matrix of intention,
calling function and substance into form.

The poet sees and speaks with words as symbols,
notes on a harmonic scale,
geometries playing on the celestial lyre
touching human hearts with compassion,
sometimes brutal, sometimes with the utmost care,
and when we sleep those self-same words
appear naked, raw, and teeming with wit
celebrating each moment and expression,
then silence and surrender followed by a golden dawn,
returning to sentience, responsibility and purpose,
communicating what must be done and what matters,
greeting each other –

"Good morning. Yes, I slept well. Did you dream?"
"The bus is delayed and rain is expected."
"Pay the bills and don't forget our dinner date."
"Don't be late!"
"And, oh yes, I love you."
"I love you too."

River of Ecstatic Poetry

A river of ecstatic poetry flows through soul and season,
from a mountain spring, just a trickle,
on the heels of storm, a torrent.
Through the wilderness, garden, or barren plane
she weaves her way with many moods speaking –
a watcher's eye apprehending every detail,
a scientist's mind defining her nature,
a lover's heart embracing the romance,
every occupation fueled with passion and delight
ascending the heights to kiss the sky.

She lingers before beginning a slow, vigilant descent,
nurtured by the past until the ocean draws her in
or the cavern consumes her, fermentation taking its toll.
She sips the elixir with sleep and dreaming to follow,
returning in a euphoric state with inspiration for the future,
like a seed gathers its forces to begin its ascent,
metamorphosis in the process, alchemy in the deed,
and poetry the language to articulate the majesty.

So it is with the soul and season,
side by side on the wings of devotion,
and we, the sensitive ones, have no option
but to bathe in this river, or die,
giving over to her moods and inclinations
expressing what intellectual beauty personifies,
You and I, poet, muse, and mystery
flowing with the current to the sea.

The Morning After

Through fields of consciousness the glass bead game plays
and entities apprehend what is happening
with constellations and geometries streaming,
leaving fiery trails and auroras to paint the atmosphere
in ethereal light, merging before our eyes.
If we have ears to hear a cosmic symphony tells it all,
resounding in human and angelic hearts
with melody in major and minor keys,
sending waves to the shore we call home.

What gifts come with age to charge us with such labor?
What shores are we approaching with treasures
that we must gather and understand?
What is in dissolution to create space for becoming,
alchemizing consciousness into form?
Who are the coalitions competing for the prize?

Will love endure, finding its place in human hearts
with expressions yet to be known on Earth?
Are the glass beads telling us that suffering
weaves with joy as symptom of a new age,
and some will make it and some will not,
with division beyond our concept of time
resolved through destiny's magic mirror?

Beloved, I hope this is worth it.
Your loneliness must have been profound
for You to light up the darkness with Your cry,
that must have shocked You with its consequence.

Art, my friend, is the wakeup call,
this love the morning after.

3

HUMAN

A Magnificent Being
Learning How To Love
With Many Masks, Roles
And Scripts To Choose
Explore and Master

My Human

My human, my Beloved,
your courage is music and inspiration for me,
recognizing evil and meeting it face to face,
disarming its adversarial, impetuous nature,
calling its name and revealing its source,
admitting that you are its host and advocate,
that in your hatred you feed its voracious appetite,
its addiction to sentience, wealth, fame, and control,
gifts and virtues in disguise,
one to know beauty and one to know worth,
one to honor and recognize the master in another,
and one to foster freedom in the human soul.

You turn a critical eye on yourself without shame,
love others as you long to be loved,
trust the universe and embrace your destiny,
trust me, your angel, guardian, and guide,
and my relations that are your relations as well,
two worlds one heartbeat keeping time,
and a third all-encompassing presence that binds.
Is not love our task and salvation
and all that we long, hope, suffer and sacrifice
simply seeds for new cycles and seasons?

My Beloved, we are closer than words can tell,
more intimate than lovers on their wedding night
consecrating their union and annihilating each other,
yet through such sentience lovers share their angels
with ecstasy that is both sublime and tragic,
temporal, fading, and dissolving in time.

We are the essence of the mystery,
yet we share the stage with beings greater than we,
and these spheres where we abide
expand like ripples to the periphery and return
with majesty that is never the same.

When you sleep I accompany you through the spheres,
returning with an afterglow, scintillating, raw,
and it takes equanimity to live the day with felicity,
meeting the challenge life brings.

My dear Human, Beloved, I love you without condition,
going where you go, willing and ready,
keeping our secrets safe, virtuous and pure,
praying that all our relations do the same,
savoring the sweetness for eons to come.

My Angel

My Angel, my Beloved,
how much time do we have in this final round
to ripen the fruit and prepare seed for the future
midst the deception preying on humankind?

Warriors stand steadfast and courageous,
shields polished to face the foe,
and evil, confronting the mirror annihilates itself
leaving devastation and chaos for amalgamation
with artists and lovers to forge a future
never known before.

In oblivion, isolated from Earth and Heaven,
there is a room where evil recovers from its labor.
Stretching its limbs, invigorated from its respite,
evil begins to dance with prodigious animation,
laughing and crying from victory and defeat.

"Defeat is such bitter joy that I seldom know."
"For eons I have defiled the good and cast it asunder
and for eons good has risen again and again,
until face to face it named me and turned away
to live in truth, beauty, and freedom,
but that is not what ended the war."
"It was in the final round when good embraced me,
speaking, 'Evil my brother, my sister, adversary and friend,
let us do this together, nurturing the garden with wisdom.'
and my power waned, transformed, alchemized,
sending me home with hope for the future."

However much time remains to complete our quest
knowing that the final round has just begun
and we must return until we are done,
let us use what we have to define our fate,
united in love that no evil can withstand.

My Angel, my Beloved,
I embrace You with love and recognition
for when You and I fade one will remain
and we will be we no more.

INVOCATION

Beloved,
it has been a long time since I invoked Your presence
using your true name,
acknowledging You as the Beloved that You are,
for all of us, Your children and lovers learning how to love,
developing capacities for being human.
Is there a difference between lover and human being?
Are we not forged from the elements,
endowed with life that You breathed into us
and soul that You conjured from the spheres
and a silver cord that connects us
and binds us in myriad geometries of space and time?

Beloved,
I know You can hear me so do not pretend to be silent.
This is an invocation, clumsy as it may be,
and although we have not mastered love
it is the only alchemy that can turn this calamity around
and get us back on course with time to enjoy the journey.
Although You say that You love us
and these times are only birth pangs and cleansing
for the glory that lies ahead,
I pray for signs that this is true,
calling for interludes so we may catch our breath
to gather courage for the final battle
that darkens the horizon and sunrise that may never come.

Beloved,
we know how our creations can return to haunt us
and wonder if it is the same with You,
if karma holds true for angelic realms as it does for us?

The course we are on appears to be out of control,
for the adversaries have forgotten their task
and threaten to enslave us,
including You, Beloved.

I stir the cauldron and add a potion
to transmute hate into love,
selfless love, without agenda or condition,
joy without fear of deception or betrayal,
wonder ever renewed without hesitation.
May all that has been conjured out of darkness
that does not beget light,
or light that does not illuminate darkness,
return to from whence they came.
Release the demons from their tasks
for they must be weary of the putrid, stagnant,
festering realms that surround them,
and last of all, cast jealousy into the fire,
for man and woman, angels and gods
have their roles, natures, and gifts.

Beloved and Lover are endowed with Love,
each within the other are the same,
for in the beginning three were conceived,
Beloved, Lover, and Love,
each the other creating, alone incomplete, and nothing,
not even presence or consciousness would exist,
only loneliness that disturbed the ominous void,
and long, long ago ceased.

Response

Beloved, You also have a voice
and when I dominate the conversation
there is no room for You to speak.
Since the beginning this has been,
with my demands, pleas, and prayers,
praise and adoration filling space, consuming time,
and since You are considerate and kind,
You listen and wait for silence to reply
with words that I may comprehend.

Therefore my voice to You I lend
and I pray that I listen well, translating with accuracy
Your truth, Beloved, and what lives within the words,
as well as the beings they embody,
that the words I choose are well chosen
to express your thoughts, feelings, and wisdom
free of filters and projection.

Your voice is song – a golden dawn, crimson sunset,
spring, summer, fall and winter, mist and rain,
a garden green with creatures everywhere,
curious and vivacious in life and love,
or wild with thunder, lightning, and wind
filling the room with you presence.

Beloved, I am here and have always been,
since that auspicious moment when it began
and I had no choice but to follow fate,
the outcome that even I cannot know.
Even though I have a goal and intention,
they are conceived from the void
from whence You, Beloved, spring.

Without You, I cannot be known or know Myself,
the ultimate riddle and conundrum.

I hear Your invocation and You are not alone.
Many have expressed in similar words this prayer,
filling worlds, reverberating through dimensions.

To be seen is love in action,
and love feeds the fires of evolution.

I, the Beloved that You are also,
the Lover whom I adore, My Beloved, My creation,
I accept My fate fostered by the desire to be seen —
as it is in the beginning, darkness lit up with light,
becoming substance from which form is forged,
the word, creation, and You.

To love we must be free
and trust, hope, and act accordingly.

We Know that You Love Us

An ancient question, I am sure,
from the beginning of time
with the cosmic dance of creation
and some righteous destiny in mind,
the mind of God or Gods, as it may be,
or angels and demons who promote evolution,
sharing the same nature and consciousness,
simply stated –

"What is going on and Why?"
More pertinent in our present state, than –
"Who am I?" or *"Why am I here?"*

We ask the question with supplication and humility
honoring Your omniscient authority.
This is not about war on Earth, freedom, or ascension,
or becoming one of You, at the bottom rung of course,
serving Your agenda, inspiring others to do the same,
until all there is, is Truth, Your Truth,
frequency specific with every cycle and transition,
and if we muster the courage to ask the question
You will most likely mirror it back to us.

Since that auspicious moment when a big bang
out of the ominous void resounded with the word,
we have been in the trenches, down and dirty,
sweating, waring, hating each other,
or loving, embracing, recognizing each other
and basking in those moments between,
timeless moments, suspended in beauty
that You will never know without us, humanity,

gazing into each other's eyes,
walking hand and hand in the garden,
smelling a rose or watching honeybees come and go,
as the sun sets upon a crimson sea
crafting liquid Sun light, Your light,
in the alchemy and assurance that You know,
declaring your love with the unspoken words –

"Forgive Me for I know what I do.
Without freedom, evolution wouldn't have a chance."
or
"The prize is not what it seems.
When you see it, nothing will bar the way."
or
"The human is in Me and We are the same.
The eye that sees is not the eye that is seen.
That one is grateful beyond measure."

Our answer before and after remains –

"We know that You love us."
"We love You too."

Praying for Grace

I go to the river and pray for grace
to meet my demons face to face.

Focusing on my breath, I breathe in deep and slow,
breathing out, steady, forgiving, letting go,
until calm comes to still the restless sea
upon which a cold wind blows,
whispering of ordeals forgotten long ago –
walking on shifting sands, hungry and alone,
losing sight of the prize with its allure,
wandering in an enchanted land without
a companion to share the adventure
or assure me that life is worth living.

Through lifetimes, cycles, and seasons I journey,
with stages and scenes to enact the script,
familiar players with entrances in perfect timing,
dimly remembering the challenge
that I must embrace and bring to fruition.

Some lovers make promises they cannot keep
betraying and clouding my vision,
and others offer love without measure
so pure that this jealous world cannot abide,
while I turn away without an explanation,
without assurance that it will come again.
If it did, would love be recognized?

I pray for courage to try once more
and surrender without compromise,
to abandon assumption and addiction
for one lifetime of sweet repose,
one lifetime veiled from dark agendas
to merge in love's presence,
sharing the joy and beauty life brings?

TRUTH AND KNOWING

What do we know about others or ourselves,
of those who pass before us on our daily round
or of the few who are near and dear,
even the most intimate, child, parent, lover,
friend or the many we adore –
a poet maybe, whose poetry opens our heart
or cracks our shell, challenging our point of view,
evoking a full-fledged revolution
that cuts deeper than any sword of steel
with the poignant, impeccable word?

Yet know them we do.
Even if the knowing is not complete
or limited by a single meeting or observation
that misses the mark by a mile or centuries,
we know with pure unadulterated accuracy
without any common scrutiny we may employ,
or that a master detective may exercise
to reveal the mystery behind the evidence,
exposing the disguise we unconsciously use
or consciously wear to evade detection.

Even if we are transparent and open
without secrets or hidden agendas,
truth as true as truth can be,
knowing is but a segment of reality,
being fixed and wrought with the limitation of time,
leading to deception, like life that flees the scene
when its host is cut open for close-up examination,
for life is always on the move and truth as well,
going somewhere and from somewhere coming,
alive in the moment without guarantee.

Maybe it is not the knowing that begs the question,
but the seeing that is wrought with error and trickery,
filtered through the seer's eye,
observation of no use in the final hour.

Yet truth and knowing thrive in every presence,
begetting an enigmatic smile of recognition.

THE IMPOSTER

I knew an imposter once.
How long ago I cannot remember,
but memories are like that, always present and timeless.
Whether it was a man or woman it does not matter,
so I will call them "they" if that works for you
and I assume that it does so let us begin.

We met by chance in an extraordinary situation
that rarely comes to one such as I,
a loner of sorts, engaged to my current occupation
for money, service, or pleasure, all the same,
and we struck up a lively conversation
about the weather and state of affairs in the world
and what could be done to set it right or make it better,
for us and everyone concerned, humanity of course,
and mother nature, animals, plants, oceans and skies,
refining frequency and vibration to alter the matrix
with a blueprint for life, love, and harmony,
followed by pact, promise, and plan to do it together,
to make a difference and have fun along the way.

For a while we were in perfect congruity,
fructifying existence with beauty,
everyone around us inspired to do the same
until dissonance slowly infiltrated the field,
like a virus that cannot be seen or analyzed.
Our friends and relations were no longer nurtured,
held or encouraged by our presence,
yet we kept up appearance and pretense
as if nothing had changed,
but it had.

They were not who I thought they were and the spell
was broken, the air crystal clear, the light blinding,
and the pain beyond endurance,
for I was betrayed by the truth that was there all along
but I could not see.

This imposter of whom I speak has been liberated
to be who they are and were meant to be,
to live an authentic life adorned in gowns of glory,
offering the world what is needed to be healthy and whole,
with no one to suspect that it has ever been otherwise,
save I who knew them once wearing an impeccable disguise,
seen through an imposter's eyes,
who may also be seen
and given another opportunity.

Voracious Life

Who am I, the I who asked this question yesterday
and found an answer or conceded to not knowing,
making excuses to still the guilt of ignorance
of the one and only answer that can free us
from the burden of personality?
If such an answer could be earned
from lifetimes of labor or in the course of a day,
would we be done or would the question reappear
with renewed vigor when we wake tomorrow?

What happens in my sleep that when I wake
yesterday's answers no longer satisfy my hunger
or protect me from error and self-serving pursuits,
stripping courage, innocence, and spontaneity
needed to perform my task and claim my calling
with integrity, authentic and sincere?

Then by grace or will I wake a second time
without selfish burdens to imprison me,
knowing that thought, feeling, and action
are wrought with error and may miss the mark,
and that the mark is not the answer,
while both are clues for who we are.

We slay the dragon with many faces
becoming human until the day is done,
with joy and sorrow the lullaby
that brings sleep, death, and surrender.
What happens then I do not know,
but when I wake a familiar voice greets me –
"Who are you today?"
"Voracious life awaits you."

Love's Uncharted Sea

Past and future stand at the threshold
debating the course of evolution,
as we retreat into Sophia's womb
to emerge as a morning star,
waiting for night to see who we are.

"Why such drama" you ask,
as we navigate through storm and season.
*"Isn't love enough to give us courage
to embrace the task and forge our freedom."*

We have one by one been chosen
and as one from one have come,
with Love seated upon the throne,
Jupiter rising in cosmic night
flooding the spheres with transformed light.

When metamorphosis runs its course
we take our places at heaven's gate,
human beings in finer forms of physicality
surrendering gravity for light born faculties of levity?

We see it all –
wheels within wheels turning,
like pendulums in perpetual motion,
a still point at extremes, a portal between,
past and future resolving their differences
while You and I in another lifetime meet
to explore Love's uncharted sea.

Equal Time for Love

How far must we go to see what is going on,
for we know that from where we stand
there is more than we can see, feel, or apprehend,
even when we shift our point of view
or expand and hone our intuition
freeing our minds of limitation?

We have a chance, as slim as it may be,
fleeting, teasing, and leading us on
through a wasteland of chaos and confusion
to the holy shrine that is hidden
in an ancient past or uncertain future,
kept alive in myth, legend, and prophecy,
a chance that gives life meaning.

No matter how much we pray,
or practice prudence and detachment,
we cannot set the quest aside,
although we come close,
grasping truth with its convictions,
or trust that needs no truth to carry on,
not satisfied with what is or has been,
performing selfless acts of kindness,
creating beauty never known before,
inspiring, healing, sharing the vision.

We are not content to allow destiny to unfold,
or abandon the desire to know what is going on
veiled in the appearance of reality,
except when we give equal time for love
and together be, in the hush,
silent and sacred.

THE RHETORICAL QUESTION

"To Be or not to Be, that is the Question."
Then I ask, *"Who wants to know?"*
Here we are again, I and I in a conversation.
I know who I am. Who are You? Another I
the same as me or are You my reflection,
both of us in search of identity?
Can You hear me? I think not because You act
as if I do not exist while You are the one asking,
so, it must be someone You address that is I,
a koan and rhetorical question?

Are You contemplating suicide, choosing *"Not to Be"*,
yet, You must know that I still *"Am"* and will be,
although in a compromised state, for We are
"Joined at the hip" so to speak.
Doing away with this body may seem a solution,
but it is like being *"Tossed from the skillet into the fire"*,
if You know what I mean, suffering another kind of death
from which it is difficult to recover.
Transformation is better.

May I suggest that You engage in artistic discipline
to expose the demons that haunt You.
Take a walk and sing to the flowers, streetlamps,
or an imaginary beloved.
Sing Your heart's song and share it with me,
the I who will always listen and seldom respond.

When you hear, *"I see that You are becoming"*,
contemplate the meaning with a light heart,
for this shall pass as well as the questions
no one can answer but You.

Longing My Mistress

What do I long to hear?
What story or tale will feed me?
Is there a poem that will free me
from the torment of my thoughts,
or are the poets silent now and barren?
Facts and figures inform my mind
but leave my soul in misery.
What can I do in such a state?

What do I long to feel
that will satisfy this hunger
satisfied to no avail many times before?
Has the muse forsaken me,
the seductress who poured the wine
and freed me from these cruel shackles?
Or is it done, the voice mute, the ear deaf,
the chamber sealed, dark and empty?

Stripped of pen, imagination and desire,
alone without friend or foe I struggle
to weather the storm, savage and relentless within.
Defying resolution I hold out for words
that speak to the heart and soul of love
without need or expectation.

When all is lived and lost
will longing my mistress remain,
vast and mysterious,
beckoning?

4

ANTIDOTE

Good and Evil Meet
Yet Neither Are The Goal
Leaving Us To Decipher
Which To Serve
And Which To Transform

Antidote

How is it with war and hate
that they dominate our destiny
and what antidote could turn the tide,
what thought rend the veil and set us free?

What tactic and demise do we meet
hidden behind the mask of truth
endorsed by wealth, fame, and authority,
that mark us doomed from birth?

Is it our subtle, sensitive minds
and our nature to believe and trust
that goodness will overcome evil
and transform fear, greed, and lust?

Is it the deeds we perform day to day
with courage, generosity, and compassion
that offer our adversaries alternatives
while realizing our goals and mission?

When it comes to war and hate
nothing worth having remains in the end,
but when embraced face to face
the adversary becomes ally and friend.

The dynamic of war and identity
lives in every human being,
in every artist with imagination,
in every deed, thought, and feeling.

What is the source of war and hate
unless it is fear of loss and rejection
that sees ownership and pride as a goal
with freedom and soul a victim?

Does not the demise of war
begin with identifying the enemy
and the mastery over hate
with naming the source of enmity?

The antidote through love is conceived
with birth and death the decisive answer.
In death identity is unmasked
and birth brings hope for the future.

WHAT WILL IT TAKE

What will it take to crack your shell,
to get through your defenses and projections,
conditioning, comfort, and self-deception
that you create along the way,
whether from this life or those before,
not that they are evil, good, moral or immoral,
and they may be beautiful begetting joy?

This "You" is not you as such but humanity,
the whole sleeping hoard that know they must wake
but put it off for one more day in fantasia,
and this "They" is We and You and I.

Self-realization is the key but not the answer,
like a word has meaning for its master and no one else,
like a poem bears a message, each to each in their turn,
knowing that one and all must be saved or all will drown.

It has been said that love is the answer,
but it cannot be seen, touched, or analyzed,
although we feel its presence, warmth and delight.

Once awake with love realized
are we done or just ready to begin
with this softening, opening, and cracking
preparation for what follows?

Healing is not the goal but a necessity
for the Jupiterian task looming before us,
to take our place with our special skill,
wielding love wrought in freedom
forged in the fires of passion and pain
experiencing what divinity cannot know
and sacrifice what we have gained
giving evolution room to grow.

Flaming Swords of Passion

We no longer stand at the threshold,
nor are we awake in this semiconscious state,
for the threshold has been shattered!
The human race is at risk,
unnoticed midst the chaos and confusion,
but the symptoms are everywhere.
Eventually the beast will reveal its evil plan,
springing onto the stage to feed on our flesh,
casting spirit into the dungeon of despair.

Can we imagine disintegration in divine worlds
that we count on to be steadfast when we are not,
when we sacrifice our freedom of thought
and cast the Arts into trivial mediocracy,
serving the enemy for money, fame, and power
with the allusion of morality?

While we can still sing our heart's song
and speak truths that inspire humankind,
let us sow seeds for future generations.

Let us act and sound the call
at the threshold once again –

"Thou Shall Not Pass!"
"Return To From Whence You Came!"
"Our Destiny Will Not Be Thwarted!"
"Our Hearts Will Not Be Tamed!"

Within this alien, inhuman flesh we plant the seed,
dormant, incubating, until that auspicious hour
when all seems lost and ill-fated defeat seems sure,
the narcissistic enemy crowing too soon,
drunk on deceit, satiated and weak.

We will return more powerful than before
with our flaming swords of passion
to claim the victory.

The Purge

What we are witnessing now is consciousness
that we have served, promoted, and embraced
since birth and before, not alone but as a wave,
nay waves upon a tumultuous sea,
swales building, cresting, breaking upon a littered beach
with garbage piled high and rotting,
putrefied, seeping into the sand,
poisoning the air and all that breathes,
life itself and the soul that births it?

Wave upon wave we explode onto the shore,
resistance weakening, barriers torn asunder,
edifices to dark lords destroyed,
purging the parasites that upon us feed,
wave upon wave with the battle cry,
deafening, sounding so all may hear –

"Surrender or Die!"
"Return to the source from whence you came."
"We no longer give you permission to enslave us,
or feed upon our flesh, soul, and spirit,
or destroy the Earth to satisfy your needs
that your home no longer provides,
your home that you did not defend
from raiders with insidious intent,
who lost their way before time's existence."

"Rule us no more for we have our work to do,
to vanquish the demons that in us reside,
to challenge the adversaries who guard the gate,
to earn the right to create life and set it free,
to love each other without condition,
to return to source the gifts we are given,
expanded and multiplied seven fold,
playful and with humor painted."

When this is done we will convene
for a celebration never known before,
laughing, dancing, and carrying on,
inviting you if you can handle such fare,
with gratitude, appreciation, and love,
lit up with levity.

Altering the Script

This life is a mystery that we live,
by choice, fate, trust, or grace,
a mystery with clues to arrange and rearrange,
built on theories with unknown endings,
inviting wisdom and other points of view
to reveal nuance we cannot see alone.

Then there is time, age, and reincarnation,
changing everything with new players coming
and those before who have established status quo
and built monuments of steel and stone
departing without a care for what they leave behind
turning their back on the chaos and confusion
that cannot be redeemed.

What might our task be with veils rent
and open to anyone, friend or foe,
stage and script set with the story underway
and few roles remaining to match our ability?

So it is, dear sisters and brothers, that we are here
not expecting or liking the state of affairs,
habits and attitudes that proliferate this world,
without choice once we have chosen.

Shall we join forces and stake our claim,
trusting intuition with grace as our guide,
living the mystery to an ineffable conclusion
in bright awareness from beginning to end,
altering the script for eons to come?

If I Had the Power

If I had the power to open the gate
for the white knight of truth and goodness
with the wise maiden of beauty and compassion,
would I dare?

With what authority could I charge such an act
of intervention and what assurance could I give
that truth, beauty, and goodness alone would enter,
forbidding others, richly dressed in seductive attire,
adversaries who promise peace, wealth, and comfort
for our freedom of choice and expression?

It is a fine line we tread when we act,
a razor's edge with an abyss on either side,
assuming that what we see is all there is,
that the consequence imagined is the only one,
that discomfort be avoided and comfort assured,
yet alone we choose and love accordingly.

Many beings inhabit this vehicle of flesh
that I call I, yet in truth is not I,
this magnificent biology generating a matrix
for consciousness to find expression
in the same vein as the source
from which we spring.

Yet open the gate we must, with discernment
for who we are and the beings we serve,
think, feel, and will into reality,
flesh and form.

LOVE RULES THE DAY

We are in the midst a ferocious storm,
trees falling when the soil no longer holds them,
sheading dead branches and live ones as well,
wind, rain, frosty meadows and cold dark morns
invading our peace and contentment.

How long will this cleanse last?
Will there be spring to follow winter?
Will there be a hush midst chaos and confusion
with sunny days and birds singing joyful songs,
flowers pushing through the debris into light,
announcing the end of war and hate,
or is it You and I who must shed the cloak of winter
and in the hush a solemn vow make?

Whatever happens we will not retreat
and when evil confronts us seek its source
striking with courage and conviction,
even if the evil is within us rooted,
even if our hearts must be revived
to love again as we did when we were young,
when we first witnessed a golden dawn,
fields lush and green with grasses swaying,
dancing with the breeze and living things agreeing
that harmony is better than blame, fear, and greed.

Antipathy and sympathy are tools for creation,
polarity playing the celestial harp,
consciousness breeding bright awareness,
for You and I are in essence human
becoming masters at the helm of fate
with swords drawn, sounding the battle cry –

"One for All and All for One!"
"Love rules the day, our victory won!"

Death and the Great Awakening

What is greater, fear of the known as it appears
or the unknown that can only be imagined,
or is fear a condition, a delusion of mind
that has nothing to do with the situation,
invoked by propaganda, deception, and lies,
with a set of rules and threats of consequence,
abduction or loss of life and liberty,
veiled with distractions, desire and need
advertised and promoted as necessity?

Is fulfillment the goal no matter the cost,
agreeing to be a cog in the machine
with pleasure or relief our reward –
a simple life, doing as told, following the rules
or not getting caught when they are broken,
surviving the world and its selfish agenda,
denying our part and projecting on others?

If fear of death is the ultimate fear,
then being dead is the ultimate solution.
Who would know if we were dead or alive
unless they could access the soul without the mask,
whether it sleeps and wakes executing its duties,
keeping up appearances and managing the senses
so they can perform their function.

When evaluation is done envision a cure
unique for every sleeping soul
with the potential to cast fear aside
with its fearful lamentations and cries.

In truth death is the other side of life
free of illusion that bears its own pain,
and dying an experience of transcendence,
the great awakening on our journey home.

A Pale Languid Moon

A pale languid moon setting in a predawn sky
with grey-black pinnacles of spruce and pine
waiting to devour her tentative hopes as they fade,
silent and wanting, like a ghost consumed in its longing.

Are we ghosts when we wake in our dreams,
haunting the halls of bygone days and passionate nights,
spending time with ghost lovers who cannot feel our touch
or hear our benediction and entreaty for reciprocation?

What resides in her shy, solicitous demure?
It could not be virtuous or innocent in her waning state.
Her longing speaks of lust and voracious hunger,
yet she bears a haunting beauty that cannot be ignored.

What calls us to her chamber without hesitation,
irresistible, leaving us without defense or immunity?
Have we always been victims, fair game for love's grace,
venturing where naivety is sure to flounder?

Are we connected, entangled, bound by declarations
made when we were young, lifetimes long, long ago,
blessed, cursed, or favored to come again and again,
hungry, hoping to be redeemed?

What do we fear if we surrender to her embrace?
What did we promise that has defined our fate
and brought us to the threshold of annihilation
to slay the dragon of selfishness and pride?

Does the moon ponder the outcome or consequence
or is she focused on the marriage and alchemy
of lovers refining their skill for selfless love,
fostering a seed, innocent and wise for the future?

We are phantoms like the moon at night
and sentient substance in the light of day,
yet within and beyond this crystal shell
there is a priceless jewel of love to share.

PROPHETS

Prophets proclaimed that false prophets would come
prophesying the future and dressed in authority,
disseminating information for impending doom,
with facts and figures to back up their claims,
pointing out problems never there before
with solutions to avoid the consequence,
becoming news that everyone needs to know.

For some life is planned and lived prophetically,
with what one needs to fit in with the crowd,
with its glamour, struggle, and destination,
to win the race and prize, latest gadgets or luxuries,
to survive in a brutal world of competition
with everyone out for themselves,
save the ones they adore and their friends,
of the same race, rank or religion.

Conflicts arise when we do not see eye to eye,
denouncing and betraying each other,
stealing the stage and claiming the leading role,
thus, many theaters arise with opposing cast and script,
the audience in the streets duking it out,
acting the drama in every aspect of life,
appearing to be virtuous with rules and regulations,
civilized, defined, and administered by fascist authority,
advanced from a primitive past where plague,
drought, and poverty were the norm.

What better focus could prophecy have than this –
layer upon layer of good and evil,
how, what, who, where, and when,
everyone looking and pointing at each other?

Until something happens through destiny or grace,
seeing things different than how they appear –
other human beings the same as I,
life a programed dream from which I am waking,
blue skies emerging, natures joys returning,
prophets, stage, and script carrying on
in a world that we seldom visit,
occupying our time with sisters and brothers,
creating a world of our choosing,
without prophecy, product, or medication.

DEATH DIVINE

How is it with war at the highest level,
amongst the gods or with the one god
who in the act of creation created duality
within the one god self that god is,
two selves at odds with each other
vying for victory, one over the other,
and balance or equanimity in a moment
that with time festers, animosity returning
more tenacious, powerful, ingenious?

Is it divine egotism we suffer,
a Faustian game with its insidious wager,
humanity and all that is on the line,
more pernicious for the warriors in the field
who wield the club, saber and word,
attacking the nature of existence
from without and within?

Do the players gain from affairs such as these,
developing tools and faculties powerful enough
to challenge the authority of the One
without conclusion or consequence known,
total annihilation, returning to the beginning
before the word, light or darkness,
before love, hate, or consciousness,
or desire for conversation and intimacy
to break the silence and nothingness
that was before the beginning?

Can we take charge and tame duality,
finding balance, give and take, love in action,
light at play and consciousness common ground
to feed and nourish All and the One?

It will not be easy, for God in duality is a fierce foe
that may not be slain in the other,
only in oneself and all the individual selves
functioning as one in sublime, authentic diversity.

Will God smile then and put the game aside
to join us who have earned love through our labor,
meeting the challenge and performing the final alchemy,
the romance, consecration, and marriage of duality?

Imagine that ecstasy, death divine.

Journey of Initiation

This poem would be too long for the page
if told line by line in its entirety, for life is that expression,
seven seals, seven trials, seven seasons in the cosmic round,
lived hour by hour through lifetimes in the halls of eternity.

Let us explore the mystery of initiation
for gods and humanity, quite similar in truth,
intricately entwined, entangled to say the least,
for one the other is destined to become,
each within the other evolving,
hierophant and disciple each other creating.

From the poet's point of view this is written,
calling initiation a journey of self, becoming,
the pure self in the trenches awakening,
like the I that I Am is source and destination.

The goal is in the field of action
and initiation simply the journey there,
casting aside what does not serve us –
guilt, greed, and shame accompanying expectation,
projection and deceit leading to resentment,
animosity and betrayal, even with our relations,
all blocking love, joy, levity, and light,
burning our house from within.

The journey can be brutal, courting despair,
unless we embrace Christos-Sophia
as guardian and companion along the way,
defeat an opportunity to transcend,
and victory nourishment for one and all,
human beings becoming, fueling destiny's fire
with a light heart and playful mind,
singing, dancing, speaking ecstatic poetry
with every gesture, gaze, and bow.

Initiation is not what it seems
and humility is not surrender.
When the prayer is answered
there is no retreat or forgetting,
no woe is me, victim or victor,
only being human and true,
accepting the task.

DOUBT

Doubt is an adversary I often meet
in the middle of the night when I wake from a dream
or restless lay thinking of events from the past,
of conversations with friends or relations,
or acts of consequence for good or ill,
and how I appeared or behaved, timid or brave,
braggard, sage, wizard or teacher
with a righteous role and point of view.

More forceful by day doubt questions my actions,
and when I have an extraordinary thought,
chastises my assumptions to do what cannot be done
because I am only human, limited, unqualified.

Doubt often hides behind the veil of perception.
Perhaps I meet someone in the course of the day,
both of us feeling an unspoken invitation,
yet, I or they pass with hello and goodbye
    because there is something to do and places to be,
the opportune moment missed
not knowing when or if we will meet again,
our intent, impatient, demanding,
while a shutter of sadness passes, forgotten.

My persona does not help to cancel doubt
but is consort in its task to bind the divine
that can dream and accomplish anything,
yet, when doubt is acknowledged as an ally,
discernment follows with insight and clarity
to claim my destiny that lives within
every thought, deed, and invitation.

Love's Moments

Time's seeming mortality stakes a claim on our soul,
as expectations fall away, unfulfilled and wanting
in a barren land of appearances and promises
made when the contract was consecrated
and the journey with its destination began.

New chapters unfold with foreboding,
the previous unresolved ones adding to the burden
until carts filled with memories linked to each other
form an endless train of disappointment and desire,
resisting the present and hiding the future
with its anticipation, bright lights and sunny days
in a haze, clinging to everything,
draining vitality so potent in the beginning,
fearless in the face of adversity
as if nothing could hinder destiny's just conclusion,
unless those promises were misunderstood,
unless the expectations were based on assumptions,
unless the purpose of being was not fulfillment,
the ending somewhere outside of time,
love's moments cherished for their beauty
and nothing more.

5

HOVERING

As Above So Below
With A Still Point Between
Watching, Patient, Present
The All Seeing I
Our Sacred Soul

HOVERING

Our stories through deeds are told,
chapter by chapter, line by line inscribed
upon the pages in the book of soul.

How naïve and innocent we are
arriving with all that has gone before,
everyone in their places,
stage, props, and mood set for a grand debut,
an incomplete script in hand,
improvisation welcome, nay, the rule,
performing our roles with fervor.

Hovering high above
we behold an intricate tapestry in the making,
warp and weft by unseen presences prepared
with us casting the shuttle.

There we are with relations, colleagues and friends,
preforming as if time was forever,
as images fade becoming memory,
phantoms of adventure and consequence
that our long journey with labor wrought.

There we are again, in the wings telling our story
remembering when we were young,
hearing stories from our elders,
of how it was for them in the beginning,
in the naiveite and innocence
essential for destiny's unfolding.

SACRED SEEDS

We come at the midnight hour
with sacred seeds to plant or keep,
without mind or heart to interfere.

Spirit guides activate a primal vow,
transcendental and bestowed with wisdom,
love's voice a whisper dissolving doubt,
the hush poignant, profound,
mighty existence beckoning to begin our decent
and no matter how many times we journey here
birth is an unprecedented adventure.

Geometries evoked from ancient tablets
create a matrix for our arrival
without a map to show the way,
hovering as we cross the threshold
and emerge into the light of day
without a voice to express our needs.

Helpless yet not alone we grow,
honing our skills and tending the seed,
this Earth that must die and be renewed,
feet firmly planted, arms upturned,
celebrating a star being born,
light to illumine the inner chamber,
light to guide us home.

ROMANCE

Romance is an enigmatic presence
with many faces and beguiling gestures,
teeming with ancient and mysterious lore,
demanding attention when she is near
and always responding to our call,
denial of no avail when she beckons,
revealing her persistent, enduring nature
once invited into a sympathetic heart.

She keeps us company from birth to death,
an essential attribute that makes us human,
and when this earthly journey begins
appears in magical, auspicious moments –
like in childhood reaching for ethereal beings
gathered around the cradle of our becoming,
or in the garden of delight playing hide and seek,
in the wonder of flowers, insects, and furry friends,
or in darkness emerging as ogre and demon.

Wonders do not fade with age
and romance thrives with her moods,
destiny pulsing in blood, thought and deed,
articulation unique for every human soul,
and lovers under her irresistible spell
surrender to the inevitable,
willingly.

LEVITY

Clouds slowly drifting, dreaming,
of what is and with grace will be
gathering for a new day's cleansing,
as the river winds its way to the sea.

We are warriors of truth and beauty,
arming new-born being with light,
for times are changing as is our duty
to love and cultivate spirit sight.

We forge the future in times of peril
while adversaries wear righteous masks,
resistance impotent and of no avail,
while upon the table lots are cast.

We wait for the votes to be counted,
with the rules of the game hidden
in a vault in fate's dark dungeon,
but we the keys have stealthily stolen.

We put in place an ingenious plan
to intervene in the new world order,
returning freedom to its stately home,
and engage in loving revolution.

The consequence cannot be known,
save that every action fuels evolution,
as gravity releases its tenacious grasp
and levity frees us at last, at last.

HOPE

Can you feel hope stirring in your soul
as the new year dreams of spring?
Can you see the Moon emerging
illuminating karma's intricate web
with a silver strand that is yours?
Can you sense the pulse within you
enkindling imaginations for the future,
compassionate, vibrant, undaunted.

Disappointment is laid aside
as broken strands of destiny mend,
inspiring a world beyond healing
where humanity and nature prosper,
nurturing each other without losing integrity,
facing mistakes with the fruit of wisdom
ripening in the warmth of the Sun.

The past is brutal, haunting, baring the door
to a future where love is the norm.

So, what is new? Haven't we said this before?
When we serve self, no one wins!
When we serve another, potential is exponential!
When desire promotes greed it gets nasty!
When we are grateful things lighten up and we can breathe!
As we become human, light and love define the weather!

Pray for clear skies, gentle rain, and abundant harvest
and make a pact to stand together, human and divine,
facing diversity without blame, guilt, or resignation,
for we are the masters in both worlds
mirroring each other.

Let's get it done, hand in hand every step of the way –
joy, life and liberty on Earth
joining with the Sun.

And so it is. Can you feel it?

THE CURSE

In my innocence I must have forgotten the curse,
or maybe it was hidden out of necessity.
No wonder resentment and disappointment remain
from the moment I became aware.

I prepared and trained for this waking hour,
imaging what it would be like
to develop my gifts and make a difference,
to heal the Earth and find solutions,
to create beauty in myriad forms and flavors,
to love, be loved, evolve and become.

Beginning and end can be felt in a moment
and what we call reality seen as illusion,
a stage for manifestation to come and go
with scenery and plot in endless variations.
You and I at center stage preform our roles
in the guise of lover, adversary, or friend,
with life and death, joy and sadness in oscillation,
past and future, cause and effect in confusion.

I pray to return to before the beginning,
before the waking that brought me here
resolute on redemption, sleeping
in the unfathomable abyss of nothingness.

I pray that we may recover our innocence
when we were the golden dawn and crimson sunset,
birdsong and magic garden, lover's kiss and abandon,
imagination becoming form, color, music, dance,
and poetry, fresh, eternal spring in all of its glory,
innocent, the curse undone as if it never was.

Clearly my heart friend this is not meant to be,
at least not simply through words or imagination.
What can we do to turn this around
or must we see this cycle to its just conclusion
preparing seeds for the future of our dreams?
What will guarantee that the seeds we plant
are the only ones and that the curse will not
sprout more insidious and tenacious than before?

If there is a future garden for love's flowers
to grow, blossom, and be in all of their glory,
shielded from hate, fear, and lust,
could we ignore the existence of the curse
thriving in some other garden?
Could it be that this is the situation on Earth
and we have been sent to enter the fray?

Even with forgetting, we must be here by choice,
with expectation and resentment of no consequence,
knowing that when our mission is complete
we will return home to our garden.

Even the question, *"Why have we forgotten?"*
does not matter in the end.

Know That I Am

Beloved, what can we say or do
to relieve your pain and satisfy your longing,
for we feel what You feel and hope each day
for love's presence alone to shine,
and dissipate ugliness, greed, fear, and hate
that imprisons humanity.

We pray for forgiveness and absolution
with another chance to right the wrongs
and alleviate the pain that lingers,
to remove the chains and open the way,
to go beyond healing and forgiveness
to claim the prize.

A gift creates an opening for a gift in return.
The honey is gold and the hive thrives with attention.
Spirit sustains us yet appears to be sustained without us.
But, is it?
Could it be that we were created to consume nature's gifts
and return them transformed, alchemized, enlightened,
creating anew what without us would not exist?
Is this "new" a necessity for life, growth, and expansion?
Without it, would what appears to be whole and thrive
wither and die?

The answer hovers, buoyant and mysterious,
embracing us, comforting us, whispering –

"I hear your prayer and benediction."
"You are my life, mystery, and reason to carry on."
"Know that I Am, forever without end."

THE HAT WALK

In a dream, I joined you on the hat walk,
others going before in ceremonial procession,
some with hats worn back exposing their radiant brow,
others with hair combed and brushed like antennae,
sensing the finer frequencies of air and ecstatic ether,
communing with supersensible entities, hovering,
enlightening the Earth and majestic mountains,
subterranean chambers and sacred pools
for inspiration and reflection.

Honoring the past with its gift and consequence,
we speak holy words, prayers to evoke spirit's intention,
giving form to substance, thought to imagination,
with the authority to love, recognizing who we are
throughout the annuals of time.

Upon sacred ground we walk, touching the Earth
that is the source from which we spring,
sensing her awareness, gratitude and adoration,
her prayer resounding as if our prayer is the same.

In a hush of recognition, thought and feeling cease.
All that remains is halleluiah, resounding still,
with the alchemical wedding only lovers know,
and in knowing birth beauty, ferocious and kind,
compassionate in its splendor.

As we walk we pray and spirit is nurtured,
fed from love burning in our hearts.
Halleluiah! Halleluiah!
Amen!

Before, During, and After

Eventually completion comes
by its own accord not encouraged
by a future state, place, or time,
and nothing remains save memory.
When memory is stilled and set aside
nothing is all there is, save You and I,
and what are we behind these all-seeing eyes
with nothing to apprehend or embrace,
save presence, insubstantial and gratified?

When the container is removed, we remain,
watching, expecting, knowing that this will pass.
When it doesn't time also meets its fate
and there is no wanting or expectation,
leaving us alone in the vast expanse
without boundary or definition.
We cannot help but laugh,
and when laughter does not sound and no one hears,
we wonder if in our dreaming we entered
a portal from which there is no return.

Try as we must there are only phantoms
beyond the veil of perception,
phantoms that know not that we are here,
phantoms that think they alone exist
and carry on as if they did, taking life seriously,
building monuments and tearing them down,
controlling a future as if it was their destiny.

We watch through the changing tides of time
fearing that we are they in our human state,
never knowing completion once creation has begun,
our only hope is that love will endure
before, during, and after.

BOUNDLESS LOVE AND PRESENCE

So much depends on the moment,
that when the moment is empty I am lost,
disoriented without content to fill the emptiness,
until I let go of the dreadful knowingness
that a time will come when dreams cease,
exhausted, silent.

No matter how much experience is procured,
how many battles won, lost, or waged to a draw,
projects pursued to their inevitable conclusion,
desire and addiction remain.

Even when drastic actions are taken to change the rules,
location, relations, stage, and narrative,
faking death and assuming new identity,
the moment urns for content worthy of pursuit,
more audacious and acute.

Even though some moments last for years
unfolding their intricate, profound appearance,
they eventually fade, exhausted, surpassed by another
with a new face to challenge the mastery of existence,
imposing greater trials for growth and transformation,
calling for focus more potent or subtle than before.

Even if the pattern could be broken
and contentment find a paradise for recreation
and a lover to dote upon returning the gesture
or friend to converse or be silent with,
without words to define or name the beauty,
to just be without time to break the mood,
would it be enough to ascend and be done?

Would a new desire take the stage
to fortify hungry hearts and inquisitive minds
with the will to go where no one has gone before,
human or divine, on Earth or in Heaven,
and beyond?

There is always more,
endings keeping time with beginnings,
graves begetting cradles, joy and sorrow at every turn,
the only possibility in the pause and hush between,
the moment hovering in boundless love and presence.

Seizing the Moment

Thirteen days and nights of Christmas
cosmic ritual of Sun, Earth, soul and spirit,
with a day out of time at the turning of time
and a pause at the moment of crossing,
past and future exchanging the baton.

The new year is consecrated with a kiss,
followed by a toast and resolutions,
the past releasing its burden,
the illusive present dancing until dawn.

Six days before and after with this one between,
twelve disciples and Christ with Sophia ever present,
twelve archetypes and the I Am in the human being,
celestial spheres imprinting a matrix
upon the tableau of the year's beginning.

On the thirteenth day the wise men come,
working their alchemy with us in the crucible,
creating an antidote at the opportune time
to meet adverasies with equanimity and grace
for the glory of the One to come.

You and I recognize each other
without ritual or resolution,
seizing the moment to simply be.

ETCHED IN LIGHT

Beloved universe of the imagination,
how beautifully you flow with time,
an invention of intellectual beauty,
leaving geometries etched in light
upon the fertile field of consciousness.

Exuberance as manifold emanations stream
from periphery to center to periphery,
with nodal points of light on the terrestrial web,
each an observer with pristine sight,
summoning consciousness in myriad patterns,
dissolving the past and pursuing a destination
that draws the infinitesimal present into view.

Geometry begets music
playing on the heart strings of our soul,
harmony and dissonance with many moods
in dissolution and amalgamation,
You and I entangled forever after,
savoring the intermissions and curtain call,
followed by bows, bouquets, and autographs.

Resonance sounds from the beginning
when the command from somewhere came –
"Let there be light to illuminate the darkness!"
fueling the fire for love's becoming,
giving meaning and joy to the journey.

Oh Beloved, how beautifully you weave light
and mold the human heart into a chalice,
freeing us to nurture life and reap the harvest
with seeds for generations to follow.

Spring

A sunny day after days of rain
followed by a day of rain again
while day by day the days grow warmer,
spring to summer followed by fall and winter,
from leaf to blossom, fruit to seed,
then sleep and dreaming of what has been,
longing to wake and begin again,
new life and inspiration, birdsong at dawn,
announcing to all living things that the Time is at Hand,
the mornings moist, teeming with potential,
followed by thoughts and feelings never felt before.

A bridge is built between worlds
as the sun and the rose beget light and love
to sustain us through the seasons,
promising life for our intentions
followed by just reward,
being, becoming, returning.

The Infinitesimal Moment

The morning mist in the predawn light
turns the world into a pearl,
whispering her enchantment –

"Stay awhile in this dream."
"You have a busy day ahead,
but the time has not come for waking."
"Stay awhile in this place between,
suspended in the hush, held and safe."

The sun with her luster
suspended in the timeless light of day,
surrenders her warmth in recognition,
and responds –

"I hear your longing and your plea,
but I also must rise and fall
with an infinitesimal moment between,
yet in that moment when we cease,
magic happens and we are free"

Beltane Eve

A Youth upon a Beltane Eve doth wander.
A Maiden in a sunlit glen awaits him.
The hour of consecration unites them.
A Soul grows ripe in a Mother's womb.

Life fuels the cosmic tides of time.
In the Sun's warmth the Soul thrives.
We tend the garden through every season.
God's creatures, once wild, are tame and kind.

A Wizard upon this Hallowed Eve doth tread.
A Witch on this moonless night walks beside him.
Souls wake from their slumber.
Love unites us forever after.

ALL SOULS DAY

All Souls Day comes round,
a nodal point of light on the cosmic wheel.

It is not the dead or living we celebrate,
but the communion of souls that together journey
in human becoming and divine awakening.

As the hallowed light draws near, veils grow thin,
and souls are freed from their sheaths.
We appear as a dream, remembering –
dancing through meadows of delight,
meeting on fields of confrontation,
working out karma, polishing the mirror,
celebrating victory and defeat.

The stars speak so we can hear
in a language more sublime and of a finer essence
than breath or thought, of what has been or will be,
and we know that our sheaths and theirs
are of the same ethereal substance that love is made of.
In this sanctified state music resounds
and we are carried on the breath of light,
and we are seen and the seer is us.

I place a candle on the altar
with your picture in my heart,
radiant, glowing, as you were in life,
smiling, anticipating our reunion,
without barrier or hesitation.

It Must Be So

I am looking at the Moon.
Is She looking at me?

I am asking the question.
Is She asking it too?

What a moment when two come together in a gaze.
How can I help but smile in recognition.
Is She smiling too?

When we touch warm sensations rise in me.
Does She feel it too?

Did She wink?
I think so, because I am winking too.

Is there a golden thread between us?
Must be, because I can see it.
Does She see it too?

Is She my reflection with a golden glow,
or am I Hers?
How can I know?

Does it matter without another to answer these questions
with answers that neither can know?

Without the knowing we know none the less
that it must be so.

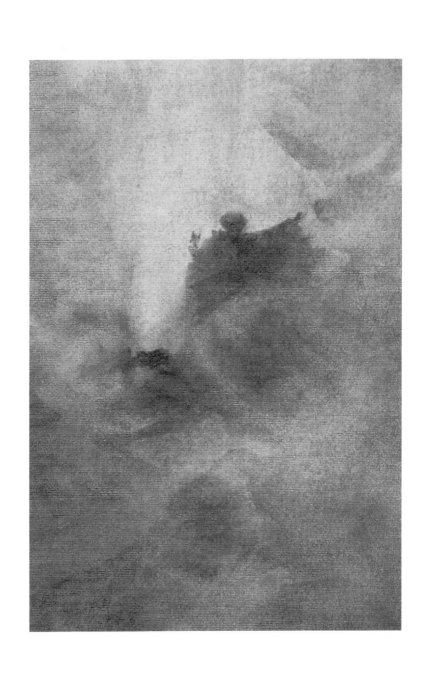

6

AGE

Time Is A Musician
Number, Pulse, Harmony
Accompanying Us
From Birth To Death
With Innocence and Wisdom
Our Benefactor

AGE

For Age to speak is granted to a chosen few,
the story on the cusp of myth and legend,
given a single page for a monumental task.

Age begins with youth, a lifelong friend,
who wakes each morning in bright expectation,
every moment new, teeming with wonder,
year by year creating a list of victories and defeats,
with completions still to be done,
opportunities missed, love lost and won,
wishing they could be lived again,
knowing that it would be the same.

Age into the murky mirror looks,
and looking back is a wrinkled face,
hair thin and white as snow,
yet a light shines in those ancient eyes
telling all that needs be told,
where choice and action were companions,
serving truth as if it was the target,
rather than soul that truth is bound to serve.

If grace was not the master behind the scenes
keeping destiny on its course,
naught that was done would be of value,
with gold still in its leaden state
and light in the darkness mute,
while You and I would have never met
to celebrate the seasons, spring's youth,
summer's warmth and winter's intimacy
wrapped in each other's arms
with gratitude for life and memory.

The Golden Dawn

Could the pain our heart suffers
and the disappointment we endure
be our greatest gift and challenge,
inspiring the progression of the story
from birth to death with celebration after?

Could it be that poetry keeps us company
in realms of heart, soul, and mind,
guiding us step by step through landscapes
with similar moods and terrain,
every deed a quest for knowledge
with grace begetting magnanimity?

Could it be that poet and muse meet early
inspiring romance through the seasons,
times changing like the weather,
sometimes sunny, warm, and fragrant
with gentle breezes and peaceful days,
or tempestuous wind, storm, rain, and thunder,
with dry, dismal, long drawn out summers?

Winters are no less ominous for the soul,
warm and cozy fires burning in our house,
snow and the great white silence without,
long nights and misty days for musing,
with age adrift in reverie.

The past is etched upon the windowpane,
with joy on our lips and gratitude in our hearts,
pulsing with ardor for life and loving,
a golden dawn silhouetting horizons yet to come.

THE DAILY ROUND

What a blessing to be old
with promises to keep and plans for the future,
yet there were times when thwarted I wondered,
when things did not go according to plan,
when friends abandoned me without explanation,
when lovers betrayed me for another
and alone I confronted the demon doubt
until the tides turned in my favor.

I remember the journey, remember it well –
a goddess joined me along the way
with children briming in expectation,
chapter by chapter the saga unfolding
without time to question the future,
without time to honor pain,
joy coming with life or no joy at all,
alchemy my occupation, the muse in disguise,
unseen yet present, beautiful, and wise,
courting addiction in ecstasy and desire,
death an ever present councilor and guide,
trials reappearing with a different face,
taking their toll with consequence.

With victory or loss there is gain,
with death life follows,
despair is accompanied with hope,
assumption with disappointment and shame,
for the pendulum swings and pulse quickens
as we sleep, wake, and sleep again,
what is above is below, what is within, without,
until a quintessential observer we become
with harmony and dissonance entwined.

When it gets down to being human
I wonder what tomorrow will bring,
with age growing thin, sleepy, and crystalized,
while today is always a happening,
like dawn and dusk never come and go,
but simply make their daily round
without beginning or end.

VINTAGE

How is it that we come to this land?
Is it chance or genius that brings us here?
What shall we do when we grow old?
How should we act?

Occupations we know are rooted in a distant past,
outdated, no longer needed or of value,
of small consequence, worn beyond repair.
But repair them we must, or transform them
with courage and audacious intent.

How is it with things when it is time to pass them on?
Even if they are refurbished, teeming with potential,
boasting the mastery and skill of their creator,
eventually they will become decor,
or traded for newer models in vogue and esteemed,
or placed in dilapidated sheds with spiders and rats.

Will anyone want them or see their enduring value
beneath the cobwebs, grime, and peeling paint,
hiding the memories of being treasured
with necessity and delight?

What are those memories worth?
Is the genius in them worth preserving
or their story worth remembering?
Is the art in the object, concept, or deed,
or is it a passing fashion to be tossed aside
in the wake of new pursuits.

And I, ancient as this,
once in my prime, desired and pursued,
am I worth preserving, kept alive until my final breath
and beyond becoming legacy?

Or is being enough,
passing on and returning as a newer model,
pristine, of eminent use, a necessity for evolution?

The Unasked Question

Did you read the poem?
It is an answer to your question
that ordinary words will not serve.
You say that you did not ask a question, yet,
your emphatic - *"I am stuck!"* foreshadows the question,
slipping out in an enigmatic moment
when your guard was down and you shared your secret
that you had not found a voice or words to speak
or admit into awareness.
You know that it must be answered or slain,
cast beneath your feet and held fast.

The question may have come when you were young
and day to day necessity held you in the current,
the eddies increasing with age,
the river diminished or retreating underground,
flowing with more urgency than before,
meandering and even stagnant at times,
inviting a flood to clean the muck and memories
that collect in pools of unrequited reflection.

What is the question or is there more than one,
the many that are one, the essential and only one?
"Why am I still here?"

"I am old and every road has been taken,
every task completed or abandoned,
yet I am still alive, stuck!"
"There, I have said it,
weather in fear of failure, unworthiness, or success,
or fear of polluting an already polluted river
that will continue to flow when I am gone."

"There must be a task or deed to be done
that no one can do but me, a story, poem, or song
that age may leave for generations to follow,
authentic and free without moral obligation,
perspectives that youth cannot see or apprehend,
a gift that age cultivates while youth is living life
to its fullest without compromise or restraint."

The answer can only be witnessed through action
in the glory of every generation
that revolution, artistic deed, and romance bring,
in the love for humanity no matter who they are,
never giving up on hope and redemption,
no matter how bleak and miserable life may seem,
summoning beauty and balance at every turn,
and when this is challenged finding nature,
vast or minute with its delicious wonders,
and when desperate, leaving all aside,
spending time with the unspeakable,
nameless, pure, radiant, auspicious, selfless self
that we are, returning vitalized.

Trust destiny until you are done,
giving the gifts that only you can give,
and do what you cannot not do,
answering the unasked question.

Claiming Our Birthright

I am old, grey, thin, and slow,
and others like me, slightly bent,
stiff and lame are old as well,
while youth sleeps and dreams
as if the world has lost its vigor,
animated without delight or aspiration,
life's treasures and beauty stored in vaults
and damp, moldy, haunted cellars,
love expensive with addiction and consequence.

This world was compromised when we were born,
performing on a stage as if life was real,
adventure, thrill, and romance at its beckoning,
a twist of the wrist and nothing more,
digits for reality, wonder waning wrung out and dry,
much different from the youth I remember.

The sleeping world where we now abide
doesn't breathe the sweet air of freedom,
walk away from wealth and fame
or wear flowers in long, unbraided hair,
or dance naked in the rain,
kissing and giving all in the moment,
birthing children with hope for the future.

Now I am old in a delicious riot of reverie
while so many seem drugged or hypnotized,
stripped of youth, lost and forgotten
without courage to take chances with fate,
winning the battle and breaking free,
alone without hope and sinking fast.

Age, however, can wake youth
with stories that cannot be dreamt,
beauty without virtue or illusion,
truth without conviction or deceit,
love without barter and free for giving
as we claim our birthright –
health, choice, and friendship
without measure.

Dreams Worth Having

Sometimes I wake sad without knowing why,
wondering if it was something I ate
or because the predawn sky is bleak,
forecasting another dark, misty, moody day
that far outnumber the sunny ones.

Maybe I brought a dream with me,
better forgotten than remembered,
demanding recognition or at least consideration
that I am living in denial presenting a happy face
and responding when asked –

"Everything is excellent and all is well."
"I am engaged in great endeavors, writing poetry
that I will publish soon, and planning trips abroad
or perhaps into town to buy a peach or two."
"I am feeling fit and walking every day."

Not mentioning that it is only to the gate and back,
resting on the old moss covered bench halfway between
to catch my breath and still my beating heart,
and muse on the bare, desolate trees
without hope or hint of life, joy, or spring.

Maybe I am growing old and can hide it no longer,
making plans that can never be carried out,
or imagining occupations that were the glory of my youth,
that even if they could be repeated
would only support my fear of the inevitable.

I think of opportunities missed and things left undone,
with the hour growing late, too late to begin again,
new relationships or old ones revisited to no avail,
for there is not enough time for completion,
to plant a garden and reap the harvest,
or bake a pie with sugar coated frosting,
not enough of anything worthwhile.

This sadness shall pass, yet it will do for now
and maybe if I live another day
the sky will be blue and the sun return
with dreams worth having.

Isn't Love Enough

I am waiting. *For what?*
For a message, I think. I am not sure.

From where does it come and who is the messenger?
It is not clear with so many questions
and answers that don't fit.

It is like a vessel that longs to be filled
and even a drop would be enough
to quench the thirst of a beggar such as I.

Beggar, my dear, do you have nothing more to give,
labor, companionship, or goods of some kind
that a benefactor may need or desire?

I have been a miner, mining for gold
but found only lead and unyielding stone.
I have been a vagrant sifting through rubbish
and nothing of value has come to my hand.

Have you tried the trades or mastered a skill
for money, barter, or recompense?

Indeed, many arts I have mastered,
creating beautiful things and inventions by the score
to serve the needs of others and bring them joy,
comfort, and inspiration.

I have been a healer, teacher, musician and friend,
landlord and lawyer with a compassionate heart,
banker and politician requiring no interest
or favors in return, performing my duties
with integrity and honor.

Now I am old and these talents are no longer
at my command.

My life is simple. I am warm and well fed.
I live with my family who love me dearly,
sharing their lives, caring for my needs.

So what is the problem?
Isn't love enough?

Dear Earth Mother

Blessed Be Dear Earth Mother,
Mother in every caress and gesture,
in touch and whisper becoming song,
soft and reassuring that all is well,
rocking as I nestle close to her breast,
her heart pulsing, waves gently washing,
informing me as I sleep, wake, and sleep again.

Day by day I am encouraged to take up my staff,
fearless in innocence to welcome the angels in,
confirming that tedious, indelible connection.
Week by week I watch and discern,
as shadows take on form and identity,
recognized as beings who bless and protect,
freeing me for life as I will grow to know it,
with bright awareness upright and speaking
truth that I am yet to conceive,
until I own the voice within, claiming autonomy.

Mother looks on as I grow and explore
month by month through the seasons,
year by year embracing destiny's revelations,
until the time arrives for me to stand alone,
Mother older now, ensouled and gentle still,
having released me with a golden thread
confirming the bond that will always be.

As I become a Mother I carry Her with me,
Her skill, presence, touch and warm embrace
firmly rooted in life's etheric rhythms.

Whether man or woman Mother's blessing flows
with tears and laughter, joy and sorrow,
every Mother with a Mother to hold her
in loving arms and eternal wisdom.

COSMIC PULSE AND EARTHLY RHYTHM

Mysterious time, perpetual or profane,
is laid out in hours, days, and years,
cycles within cycles, tangible or imagined,
with continuity in past and future,
necessity and freedom in the present,
boasting reasons why with effect added on,
and something deeper bleeding through
with names and identity for our journey,
revealing who we are or appear to be
as participants in story, myth, and legend.

This "time" of which we speak and use
to plan our lives and mark our days
defies manipulation, like light, space, or love,
enigmatic, denying access to the mystery.

Time is so much entwined in our world,
in breath and heartbeat, tides and seasons,
in music, poetry, and the spoken word,
animating expression, thought and narrative,
that without it we would not exist.

The spiral of time unfolds,
persons, places, and events appearing with agendas,
nodal points of light on the strand of past and future,
a map for mind, heart, and deed to perform their task
with consequence that must be lived,
passing in review before the ever present eye
with freedom to choose and create.

Time, my friend, is a muse
inspiring us to live life with tenacity and wit,
traveling the labyrinth from periphery to center,
cosmic pulse and earthly rhythm
keeping us company.

Age Comes Once More

Age comes once more to my room.
With tears and laughter I tell my story,
chapter by chapter through the seasons,
the conclusion lingering in the wings.

Heartfelt questions were answered along the way,
poetry and muse my faithful companions,
and lovers, oh my, lovers, just a few,
chosen to open my heart and strip me naked,
my soul on the altar of sacrifice and dissolution,
leaving anticipation with its projections behind,
residue lingering, praying for freedom.

Essential questions that brought age here remain –
"Why am I still alive, blessed with grace as my guide,
near death experiences stripping away ego and pride,
enfolding layers of soul on the anvil of victory and defeat?"
"Why am I different, accepted but never quite fitting in,
as if riding a wave to a foreign shore?"
"Why does inspiration and insight come without the skill
and grace to share them with others?"
"Why do I have these healing hands if they cannot touch
another soul without expectation or condition?"
"Why does love fill my cup to overflowing
while I am unable to fill the cup of others?"
"What must I do now to fortify life's legacy?"

Maybe before I go, just maybe,
there is joy in the wings yet to be embraced
with unexplored encounters and intimacies.

"Satisfaction in never guaranteed!"

Moon and Loom

A full Moon on the cusp of dawn
reveals night's intentions for the day to come,
and not fully formed bring with them
secrets born in heaven hidden from the Sun
that lays bare every motive and action
known by mind, heart, and hand.

These secrets once a month appear
at the end of night when the Moon is full
a cycle thirteen times a year completing,
year by year a story into the fabric weaving.

It is this tapestry human beings weave,
never complete yet refined with age,
youth fading, wan, tattered and thin
with meticulous years to follow,
the tapestry filled out but still not done,
still upon the loom when wizened hands
no longer control warp, weft, and weave
with dexterity, rule, and measure.

The secret now is clearly present
until pieces in the puzzle find their place,
the secret, secret no more,
appearing each month when the Sun has set
and a full Moon rises in the East,
the loom silent now,
hands at rest and our soul free
to bathe in the mystery
until dawn and day return.

Welcoming Home

So it is with age
that life becomes rich,
vast in an expanding inner universe,
recognizing others,
dancing with the Beloveds,
in dreams,
in poetry,
in moments of bright awareness
with the veil growing thin,
transparent,
opening to the mystery,
welcoming home.

7

HOME

Space and Time
Destination and Departure
Threshold, Hearth, and Harbor
Love, Lover, Beloved
Human and Divine

Gossamer Wings

Some of us wonder as we wander,

"Where are we going and what is our destination?"

It may not be clear but it seems we are going somewhere.
Many of us have a goal and destination in mind
or even a plan of how to get there and what it will be like.
Some imagine completion to be a pause, an interlude,
before new goals are imagined and embraced,
on the road again, engaged in occupations and projects
that day by day, months or years seem endless,
and even if there is life after death is it a destination
or is there more?

Novalis, dear poet, scribed this for us to ponder –

"Where are we going then? Always towards home."

Thus we wonder as we wander what it will be like
when we arrive at this place called home
and then are we done, finished, satisfied?

Picture the people and events in your past.
Remember your goals and situation.
Did they unfold as you planed?
Are you home or still homeless, returning,
or is home with you and you never left?

Is it the destination that matters
or the getting there that gives life meaning,
or more poignant, is death a destination
and once dead, rebirth the goal?

Are we not back to the primal wondering,
smiling at the thought and rolling in wit,
with mystery an adventure conjuring the future,
and home the destination and point of departure?

Do you get the point or do you care?

While you contemplate this,
may I suggest that you live life to its fullest,
lit up with possibility and love along the way,
eventually emerging from the chrysalis
with gossamer wings of wonder and delight,
or maybe you already have.

What a blessing!

WITHOUT END

Three tables before the grail each equal to twenty-one,
then forty-two and sixty-three,
birth, life, and death unfolding,
story, legend, and myth beholding,
God, Goddess, You and I with the music dancing,
three by three, seven by seven keeping time,
each to each a portal for initiation,
destiny, choice, and acts of will revealing,
from ethereal space to crystalline form,
three in one, one in three through us playing
upon a stage, earth, air, sea, and sun,
cycles imbued with rhythm, pulsing, looping,
geometries with life on Earth weaving,
gifts to accept, own, and make known,
each new, lit up and fading, returning to source
for a just review, wiser and with wisdom crowned,
signing up for another round.

What a miraculous story this journey tells,
You and I exchanging places along the way,
embracing our roles with courage and gusto,
free to choose, live, and create,
every scene, act, and performance an adventure
as we wake, sleep, dream, and wake again,
never bored and always challenged.

We fashion constellations with our friends,
liquid will and cosmic iron in our veins,
grail and blood seven years in the making,
woven into sword, scepter, and crown,
You and I each other serving.

We celebrate life and its simple pleasures,
generating beauty, story, and song,
light filled days and star spangled nights,
high mountain meadows teeming with flowers,
fertile gardens that we were born to tend,
initiation neither goal nor completion
but what comes before, after, and between,
Love, Lover, and Beloved without end.

Defining Home

Do not hurry. Do not terry. Contemplation serves both.
Within our being is the healing, source the destination.
Give it all to all in need and spirit being feed.
Death begets life, a gift for a gift, each to each returning.
The dragon breathes light by day
and lights up the night with diamonds.

We come and go, each life more refined,
weaving strands for destiny, brewing fine red wine,
becoming conscious in body, soul, and spirit,
an open mind and heart for every season,
inspired by possibility without doubt,
intuition freeing us for ascension.

Others who have tread this path before
evolving to a more conscious state
accompany us on our journey,
opening the window to reveal the mystery
with hearts of love for consecration,
thought and feeling to hone our vision,
ethereal bodies of pearl, eyes of emerald,
hands of light, breath the grail,
the sweet Earth fluid and alive,
substance no longer needed to feed us,
war no longer needed to wake us,
death no longer needed to liberate us
with an imagination to define home.

MAYBE JUST MAYBE

Liftoff and looking down at my life,
grateful for what is and sad for what could have been –
You and I leaving our karma for another time,
and maybe, just maybe going beyond the necessity
of being the other's adversary on this human journey
of transformation to higher states of consciousness,
as courage and grace shatter expectation
surrendering to the moment without consequence,
finding beauty in everything and everything beautiful,
becoming what we cannot realize but in our hearts desire
and in the aftermath trusting the universe,
remembering how to love.

However, under the circumstance this is a lot to ask
and maybe it is better to leave things as they are,
to simply do our best, planting seeds for another life,
another chance to love without agenda.

Maybe you can feel what I mean or am trying to say –
that I love You beyond appearance and need,
and maybe it isn't on Earth in bodies we experience this,
and maybe, just maybe, it is.

How Does It Go Beloved

How does it go Beloved, this mischief and deceit,
placing everything in question, even You,
whose image long ago faded into memory
of dew covered fields sparkling in sunlight,
flowers, red, violet, and gold peeking through the grass,
ethereal, like a mirage on a hot summer day,
and a sweet breeze, yes sweet, caressing the senses?
Your beauty and alure intoxicate the moment
as birds, enchanted by Your presence sing,
hoping about in unrestrained joy for life, air, and wing,
and bees making their rounds spread the elixir
ensuring future springs for eons to come.

We both know that this is temporary
although Your time is different from ours.
With mercy and compassion You love us
more than Yourself that long ago was sacrificed
for an ideal, a vision of balance with duality,
and the third original One envisioned as well,
for a propitious outcome where love will endure
from evolution to evolution throughout time.

All we have is the moment, the impeccable present,
to love a true love, human beings that we are
in our corporality, sensual and sentimental,
romantic and brazen without fear of the outcome,
as long as we do not know the truth,
and that does not bode well for us Beloved,
innocence waning with every experience,
with every broken heart and betrayal.

Beloved, is it true that eventually we will be alone,
abandoned in a dark world withering from neglect,
torn apart by jealousy, bartering for glory and fame,
or is there a final purging soon at hand
that will give us, Your lovers Beloved,
another chance to love with joy the victor?

But we know this is only possible for a moment
and if we evolve into a Oneness that is You,
the destiny of pure love,
we will cease to exist and You also.

Can either of us endure such pain or ecstasy,
utter and absolute annihilation?

THE TWILIGHT HOUR

There is a place I go when the world is still,
in winter when the wind does not blow,
and there I ponder my life with its adventures
and the long journey that brought me here,
the mistakes I made and opportunities missed,
things that I could have done or not at all,
friends and lovers that I loved and who loved me,
and in the end were betrayed or abandoned
for some quest, while many unmet remained.

Alone I sit by the sea and wait
for the Sun to set on a distant shore,
sit and wait patiently in that twilight hour,
when neither light nor dark claims a victory,
and as I, seems to be wrought with reverie.

In winter when all about me sleeps
I sense a quickening with anticipation
for spring that is sure to come,
and even though my long life is spent
and I am a husk of what I once was
in those glory days of summer
when I performed heroic deeds
and placed plaques upon now yellowed walls,
I dream and pray for another opportunity
to travel the royal road with serenity and grace,
this time not alone but in good company,
this time listening before I think and act
without claiming the task as mine alone,
this time with love and compassion as my guide
and temperance as my master.

And one more thing I ask –
for You, Beloved, to be with me in the twilight hour
and witness the Sun in its glory
opening the door to our heavenly home.

Predator And Prey

Within each of us a lion sleeps and wakes,
roaming the vast planes of existence,
alone, present, alert with every fiber of her being,
aware of the subtle nuance in the wind
bearing scent and essence from predator and prey,
efficacy drawn from the sinew of elemental worlds,
watching, waiting, listening,
while the landscape changes day into night
and the pride gathers for warmth and intimacy
giving over to dreams deeper than any well.

Between Heaven and Earth the lion keeps her vigil,
courageous, willing, and savoring life with its luster,
the Sun at midday tending Her flock,
steadfast in the quest for balance
with destiny's rhythms keeping time.

This Sun shines in us as well,
warming our hearts, enlivening our souls,
consciousness streaming from her radiant orb,
while angels, steadfast and dedicated, watch over us.

You and I at the center where periphery meets
are transformed in the fire of creation
and sustained by the passion for life,
giving us courage to come again and again,
predator and prey annihilating each other.

As it is in life so it is in death,
savoring the sweetness from the fruits of our labor,
enduring the dry, arid fields of selfishness
followed by rest and recreation in loneliness or bliss
with hearts like mirrors burning in a midday Sun,
reflecting the starry night in all of its glory.

Pristine Shores

Is it simply the lack of light that brings the night,
or the death of darkness that brings the day,
or something more elegant, like love that births a star?

A creator resides in every creation, in every breath
a cosmos spanning the sky, illuminating the majesty,
You and I with eyes to see beauty everywhere
and when we do, Eureka, Eureka,
and nothing, nothing is the same again.

What a blessing, what grace when it comes.
If not now, then when,
in another life if we are lucky
as if luck is a trump for fate,
or maybe we will have another chance
emerging in another time, another form?

And You and I, what of us –
still adversaries who cannot trust
or rise above this corporeal state to Epiphany,
our birthright to awaken to who we are,
as it is in the beginning without end,
living in the present, lit up and inspired,
loving without labor, need, or intention?

Although we may not know how to behave
in this virtuous and hallowed state
surrendering to love and sharing a star,
we offer a prayer to light up the night,
forgiving the darkness that eclipses the day,
and journey together sharing our gifts,
with a river of grace blessing all living things,
carrying us home to pristine shores.

The Illusive It

Did you get It?
Was It spoken so that you could grasp It,
word for word so others may follow suit
with details to rearrange for appearance
and information in continuous flow,
pushing the boundaries, the depths and heights,
the minute and vast with what lies beyond,
unknown but definable with metaphoric wit,
common language to express the illusive "It"?

Coy and beautiful, It has intelligence,
always a step ahead enticing you to follow,
somewhere that is unclear but somewhere for sure
until exhausted you put It to rest,
cleaning up the residue, broken promises
with myriad unresolved relationships,
volumes of exhortations artistic and wise
while institutions control and thrive,
claiming existence to be rooted in fact,
your name in the appendix and nothing more.

Long ago It became your adversary and friend,
accompanying you every step of the way.
When inspiration became dry, tasteless, and grey,
when doubt and complacency met you at every turn
with death, dying, and disintegration your reward,
It was undaunted, steadfast, always there.

It is up to you to claim your power,
freeing yourself to explore Its mysterious shores
with occupations fit for body, soul, and spirit,
meeting your trials with perseverance,
reciting poetry in the light of a crescent moon,
caressing your naked, innocent mind,
alive and raw.

So, if you do not get It, all the better.
It cannot be got!

You will see, dear friend,
the mystery profane and sacred is within you.
You and It are the same.

Pun or koan, It does not matter.

HOME IS WHERE LOVE IS

Endings are difficult as well as goodbyes,
whether you are the reader expecting a conclusion
that offers possibilities for the future,
or the writer challenged with completion,
aware of the readers expectations
and wanting to satisfy or slay the dragon
of contentment or feel-good desire
that many humans pursue.

Assuming that you have been present
in a linear fashion from beginning to end,
then completion is a kind and honorable gesture,
but we know life does not work that way
for most of us.

Time is more dynamic than we think,
appearing to begin and end with a between
where we live, exist, and grow.

Then there is another side of time
that seems dormant, suspended, incubating,
but that is not where we are at
in the act of writing and reading.

What is clear is that there are at least two worlds
and they are entangled with time and space,
a poem in action with romance teeming,
or raw observation, freezing both.
How boring!

Well, my friend, this too must end
and I wonder how You feel in this state?
As for me, I am grateful for this opportunity
to be the poet sharing these musings with You.
And now I cannot find an end!

This goodbye is not working!
Listen! The muse is laughing at us –

"Haven't you understood any of this?"
"Home is where love is and all there is, is love."
"I love You and that is all there is to It."
"Oh snickers, words do not suffice,
but the page ends, so there!"
"Have a beautiful life."

Arriving Home

Are you wearing a curious grin,
not quite laughing and rolling your eyes
as if someone is watching and you could care less,
returning their gaze and smiling more,
nodding and shaking your head in disbelief
that this magic carpet is nearing home,
not quite the same as when it departed?

Maybe you are not the same person,
yet the one laughing or chiding me is genuine
and when the one watching your reactions,
the one you cannot see, the mysterious one,
gets your attention, eye to eye,
you smile again, questioning your sanity,
wondering if you are arriving or never left,
or if home has been with you all along,
keeping company with the ever present watcher,
closing this book, done with its nonsense.

If by chance you open it again
it will be different, even the magic carpet
will have a different warp, weft, and weave.
Yet something will be the same.

It is that something, that formless presence
that is the point of these mad musings,
as well as this love You and I share
and cannot see.

Her True Name

In an infinitesimal moment it happened.
I was sitting on a moss covered log by the river
listening to a cacophony of voices rising from the water
as it tumbled over stones with unusual enthusiasm
that comes with spring, longer days, and warmth,
teeming with vitality, drawing me in.

It seemed that I was the river,
sensation and sound everywhere,
one voice and many voices throbbing
with delicate, playful melody from which
Her name came, faded and came again,
singing to me as if I was a child,
enraptured, awake for the first time.

Amma Maria Magdalene of the Waters,
of Earth, Air, Fire, and Aether…

I am Amma Maria Magdalene…
I am, I am You, I am everything, everywhere, I am I…

When I returned the river was still there
singing her joyful song.

Why is love needed now that I know?

Index Of Titles

Section 1: Place

THE PACIFIC NORTHWEST	2
THE BEACH HOUSE	4
LOVE IS ALWAYS THE PRIZE	6
DAWN AND DUSK	7
NEWBORN SUN	8
THE TEMPLE	10
THE PINNACLE	11
NIGHT IN WINTER	12
A MIDWINTER'S TALE	14
WHAT DO WE SEE	16
TOUCHING THE UNTOUCHABLE	17
THE QUEST AND GRAIL	18
WE ARE FREE	20
THE DARK NIGHT	22

Section 2: Art

ART AND ARTIST	26
IMAGINE	27
COLOR	28
STORY	30
INTELLECTUAL BEAUTY AND THE ALCHEMIST	32
THE DROP	34
SOMETIMES WHEN I PRAY	36

WHO ARE YOU BELOVED	37
BOUQUETS AND DIGITS	38
ACROSS THE THRESHOLD AND BACK AGAIN	40
NO NEED TO DREAM	42
ULTIMATE SURENDER	44
WRAPPED IN WIT	45
RIVER OF ECSTATIC POETRY	46
THE MORNING AFTER	47

Section 3: Human 49

MY HUMAN	50
MY ANGEL	52
INVOCATION	54
RESPONSE	56
WE KNOW THAT YOU LOVE US	58
PRAYING FOR GRACE	60
TRUTH AND KNOWING	62
THE IMPOSTER	64
VORACIOUS LIFE	66
LOVE'S UNCHARTED SEA	67
EQUAL TIME FOR LOVE	68
THE RHETORICAL QUESTION	69
LONGING MY MISTRESS	70

Section 4: Antidote 73

ANTIDOTE	74
WHAT WILL IT TAKE	76
FLAMING SWORDS OF PASSION	78
THE PURGE	80

ALTERING THE SCRIPT	82
IF I HAD THE POWER	83
LOVE RULES THE DAY	84
DEATH AND THE GREAT AWAKENING	86
A PALE LANGUID MOON	88
PROPHETS	90
DEATH DIVINE	92
JOURNEY OF INITIATION	94
DOUBT	96
LOVE'S MOMENTS	97

Section 5: Hovering 99

HOVERING	100
SACRED SEEDS	101
ROMANCE	102
LEVITY	103
HOPE	104
THE CURSE	106
KNOW THAT I AM	108
THE HAT WALK	109
BEFORE, DURING, AND AFTER	110
BOUNDLESS LOVE AND PRESENCE	112
SEIZING THE MOMENT	114
ETCHED IN LIGHT	115
SPRING	116
THE INFINITESIMAL MOMENT	117
BELTANE EVE	118
ALL SOULS DAY	119
IT MUST BE SO	120

Section 6: Age 123

- AGE 124
- THE GOLDEN DAWN 125
- THE DAILY ROUND 126
- VINTAGE 128
- THE UNASKED QUESTION 130
- CLAIMING OUR BIRTHRIGHT 132
- DREAMS WORTH HAVING 134
- ISN'T LOVE ENOUGH 136
- DEAR EARTH MOTHER 138
- COSMIC PULSE AND EARTHLY RHYTHM 140
- AGE COMES ONCE MORE 142
- MOON AND LOOM 143
- WELCOMING HOME 144

Section 7: Home 147

- GOSSAMER WINGS 148
- WITHOUT END 150
- DEFINING HOME 152
- MAYBE JUST MAYBE 153
- HOW DOES IT GO BELOVED 154
- THE TWILIGHT HOUR 156
- PREDATOR AND PREY 158
- PRISTINE SHORES 160
- THE ILLUSIVE IT 162
- HOME IS WHERE LOVE IS 164
- ARRIVING HOME 166
- HER TRUE NAME 167

A Conversation at the Southside Coffee Café

Good morning John. I see that you have your favorite fair, chocolate latté and a cinnamon twist. I will get mine and join you. Remember what I like?

Indeed I do, Sarah, triple shot Americano with froth on top and a sticky bun with vanilla frosting.

It has been seven years since we met at the Southside Bookstore, browsing the poetry section for something current and worth reading. Do you remember John?

I do and we have met many times since, reading the same books and talking about them over coffee or tea. You are chipper today Sarah, full of life and enthusiasm.

That's me. But I have my serious side as well as a romantic one, all too human in this digital, programed world in which we live. Coming here, I walked through the park by the lake. Flowers are in bloom with water droplets on their petals, glistening and winking at me, as if they could see me as I see them. Anyway, I wonder at things like that and they give me pleasure.

Sarah, you are a romantic no doubt. On my way here I was contemplating a mathematical anomaly about sevens, nines, and elevens and how they show up in nature and our lives, as well as in cosmic rhythms. Even numbers have their kind of romance, seemingly different from flowers. Well now Sarah, your copy of Misty Mountain Musings looks like it has been well loved with coffee stains and dogeared pages.

It is true. I carried it with me for a while, even to the beach, and wrote thoughts and musings of my own on some of the pages. I can't say that all of the poems resonate and give me comfort or amusement, pun intended. God forbid if they did! Some of them challenged my heart that wants to look on the bright side of life. Remember John, I am a romantic.

Come now Sarah, Romanticism, if that is what you call these musings, does not just look at the "bright side" but also at the dark, desperate, and evil in the world with a glimmer of hope and reprieve. I cannot say that I read all of the poems before I skipped to the end only to find our conversation recorded, somewhat accurate as I recall. Anyway, I am challenged by many of the thoughts and indications in the poetry itself. The ongoing assumption that reincarnation and karma are truths rather than beliefs. And the idea that things are somehow alive, a part of our world, observing us as we observe them. And even more absurd is the thought that what we do affects the spiritual world for good or ill or that when we die we participate in that world and this one as well. And as romantic as it may be, the imagination that we plan our life before we are born with a team of angels who weave the web of destiny in our favor is off the wall strange, although it would answer questions about my parents and who I meet in my life and even You and I having coffee in the Southside Coffee Café. Now you are laughing!

Dear John, if you could see your face, you would laugh too. I have never seen you like this because you are usually so reserved and sure. I did not notice those things so much. For me, I felt that I was empowered to be who I am and not have the world act on me, rather to engage with what is and with other human beings who love and laugh, cry and weep, and feel all kinds of emotions. Just this recognition changes everything and brings us together to act and do things in our life for the better. Don't you see John, there is hope and we are the ones to make it come true. Now you are laughing!

Sarah, I got it! Our time is at hand and this is what we were born to do. Look at me, talking like I have some kind of destiny. Muse on that!

So it is that Sarah and John leave the Southside Coffee Café hand in hand, laughing. If you could see them, you would laugh too. They look like children in grown up garb, smelling the flowers and feeding the birds, smiling at passersby who smile in return, lifting their gaze a little higher, seeing the world anew.

Then something strange happened. A young girl, six or seven years old, stopped them, pulling on John's shirt to get his attention. She looked into both of their eyes with a whimsical grin and handed them a small envelope.

"This is from the man over there on the bench under the Linden tree."

She pointed towards the bench, then curtsied and left. The man was old with long white hair that came a few inches below his shoulders. He wore a colorful loose fitting shirt,

draw string pants and sandals. He looked at them with a curious grin and a sparkle in his eyes as if to say –
'Things are not as they seem. I am the messenger and nothing more. The letter is from the Muse, as ancient as I and enchanting. It is the answer to your question –
'Is the answer enough?'"

Sara and John looked at each other as if to say –
"Did you hear what I heard?"
"Did you ask a question?"

They looked up and the old man was gone. As if in a dream they went to the bench under the Linden tree, opened the letter and read –

Dear Sarah and John. We are pleased that you found the book. It was written for you. Here is a musing that was left out until you were ready to spread you wings and soar. Love is all you need.

Is The Answer Enough

Long, long ago when rain fell from the sky
and the mountain was veiled in mist
and the fate of the green Earth was known,
we were here looking back and wondering
at the many episodes along the way,
each drawing from the one before
and leaving seeds for the ones to follow.

How did the first episode come to be with nothing
to precede it, without a seed from which to spring?
Some presence, intelligence, or consciousness

must have been the source to conceive and set
the journey in motion with purpose and destination?
If the answer could be known, is it enough?

Every answer begets a question to lure us on.
It is the nature of being and becoming.

What then is the purpose of these musings?
Don't look at me. It is your question.
Muse yourself and see what happens.
There are many potentials and outcomes.
Try beginning with the answer.

*How boring and meaningless a journey would be
without You to keep me company.*

That is a beginning.
All we need now is love and fuel for the fire.
What was the question?

The cycle is well underway and the tide is rising,
wave upon wave cresting, breaking upon the beaches
of time, steadfast and relentless, joining with friends
and relations for an Age of Love to follow.

Forget the question. The answer is enough.
Thank you for coming.

ACKNOWLEDGEMENTS

I would like to acknowledge my family, friends, and relations. Know that you are loved, appreciated, and adored. Also much gratitude for the many facilitators, presenters, and participants in global zoom gatherings and conferences hosted by the Anthroposophical Society. You have been my home and inspiration. Thank you Sally and Ami for your drawings that speak with their special voice. And finally to the readers who give this book wings.

For the past two and a half years I have participated in virtual meetings with the Literary Arts Group, originating in Fair Oaks, California for the Section for the Literary Arts and Humanities ("Beautiful Sciences") of the School for Spiritual Science in North America. Special thanks to all of you and to Bruce Donehower and Marion for your collaboration and encouragement.

Short Biographies

Nicholas Michael Morrow

"In the summer of 1943, America is engaged in WWII. My parents drive from San Diego, California to Savannah, Georgia where my father boards a ship for Germany. Ten days later my mother drives back to San Diego. We live in military housing near the sea, with its moods, tides, fragrance and foreboding, sandy beaches and narrow stairs without a landing, my first memories, alone with my imagination. From the beginning poet and muse are my companions and now in the hopeful, fateful days of twenty twenty-two they are present still."

Nicholas grew up in Texas and spent most of his life in Northern New Mexico. He was one of the founding teachers at the Hawthorne Valley Waldorf High School in New York and taught practical arts in grades six through twelve. He has been active in the arts most of his life and sees the creative process as natural and necessary for every human being.

For anyone wanting more information about this book, to share comments, view other writings or learn about Misty Mountain Arts visit mistymountainarts.com

SALLY RUTLEDGE

Sally is an artist working out of anthroposophy, with a career as a Waldorf teacher and lazure artist behind her. She lives in rural New Mexico and teaches charcoal and color classes. Website: sallyrutledge.com

AMI SPANGLER

Ami, a life-time apprentice to Goodness, Beauty, and Truth, fledged in Greenwich Village, then Connecticut and England where she encountered Anthroposophy via art and art therapy. Ami lives in Northern New Mexico where her art has become consecratory and collaborative with Gaia Sophia.

Pray

I am complete now and close.
The fear has past as if resigned,
the message no longer needed
and doubt as well set aside,
freeing life for the grand finale.

Sight is a child again,
seeing without judgement or words to tell,
but truth, oh my, truth is raw, brutal,
compassionate like beauty that proceeds the dawn,
every action preparing for what follows
with reverence for a past that is done.

Don't give up your power to trust midst the storm!
Spend time with the muse teeming with imagination
and mold the Earth into sumptuous form.

Remember when we wore flowers in our hair
and danced in meadows of delight?
I will meet you there
without boundary or hesitation.

Friends and lovers will know the truth.
That is the crisis!
Pray that we survive.

AMMA
SOPHIA

Made in the USA
Columbia, SC
08 January 2023

74922680R00111